MEDIA
POLLS IN
AMERICAN
POLITICS

MEDIA POLLS IN AMERICAN POLITICS

Thomas E. Mann and Gary R. Orren
Editors

A Study Produced Jointly with the Joan
Shorenstein Barone Center on the Press,
Politics, and Public Policy, John F. Kennedy
School of Government, Harvard University

The Brookings Institution
Washington, D.C.

Copyright © 1992
THE BROOKINGS INSTITUTION
1775 Massachusetts Avenue, N.W., Washington, D.C. 20036

Library of Congress Cataloging-in-publication data:

Media polls in American politics / Thomas E. Mann and
  Gary R. Orren, editors.
      p.   cm.
  "A study produced jointly with the Joan Shorenstein Barone
Center on the Press, Politics, and Public Policy of the John F.
Kennedy School of Government, Harvard University."
  Includes bibliographical references and index.
  ISBN 0-8157-5456-6   ISBN 0-8157-5455-8 (pbk.)
  1. Public opinion polls. 2. Public opinion—United
States. 3. Election forecasting—United States. 4. Mass me-
dia—Political aspects—United States. 5. Press and politics—
United States. I. Mann, Thomas E. II. Orren, Gary R.
III. Joan Shorenstein Barone Center on the Press, Politics,
and Public Policy.
HM261.M44 1992   92-27869
303.3'8—dc20   CIP

9 8 7 6 5 4 3 2 1

Foreword

IN THE PAST thirty years, public opinion polls have become staples of contemporary political reporting. Indeed, polls often seem to dominate coverage of campaigns and elections, producing incessant attention to the candidates' standing in the race and to their strategy and tactics. The unhappiness of many Americans about elections is increasingly reflected in the widespread concern that the proliferation of polls threatens to undermine the democratic dialogue between citizens and their leaders.

Yet media polls—properly conducted, analyzed, and presented—can increase the independence and quality of news reporting and give the public a chance to help set the agenda of campaigns and define the meaning of elections. The editors of this volume contend that media polls can be a constructive part of American public life but only if they are used to help report news, not create it.

This volume is a joint product of the Brookings Institution and the Joan Shorenstein Barone Center on the Press, Politics, and Public Policy, John F. Kennedy School of Government, Harvard University. The idea for the volume grew out of a conference on the use and misuse of polls convened in 1989 by the Shorenstein Barone Center. The editors, Thomas E. Mann, director of the Governmental Studies program and the W. Averell Harriman Chair in American Governance at Brookings, and Gary R. Orren, professor of public policy at the Kennedy School and associate director of the Shorenstein Barone Center, recruited a group of polling experts from academic and news organizations to examine the proliferation of media polls, the influence of technology, sources of error, variability in poll results, and the impact of polls on the public, reporters, and the state of American democracy.

Contributors included John Benson, the Roper Center; Henry E. Brady, University of California, Berkeley; E. J. Dionne, Jr., *The Washington Post*; Kathleen A. Frankovic, CBS News; Michael R. Kagay, *The New*

York Times; Everett Carll Ladd, University of Connecticut; and Michael W. Traugott, University of Michigan.

The editors would like to thank Marvin Kalb, Karlyn Keene, and Richard Morin for their advice. James Schneider edited the manuscript. Secretarial assistance was provided by Susan J. Thompson and Elizabeth O. Toy. The manuscript was verified by Alison M. Rimsky and prepared for publication by Susan Woollen. Julia Petrakis prepared the index.

The Shorenstein Barone Center received support for the project from the Goldsmith-Greenfield Foundation. Brookings would like to acknowledge support for this project from the Cissy Patterson Trust.

The views expressed in this book are those of the authors and should not be ascribed to the sponsors of the conference or the trustees, officers, or staff members of the Brookings Institution.

Washington, D.C.   Bruce K. MacLaury
August 1992   *President*

Contents

Chapter 1

To Poll or Not to Poll . . . and Other Questions

THOMAS E. MANN AND GARY R. ORREN

To POLL or not to poll is almost never the question. Polls have become ubiquitous, a hallmark of contemporary politics. No person or organization wants to do battle without polling as a ready weapon. This is true for public officials, political candidates, and interest groups, and it is also true for journalists. Polls, which are an indispensable technology in the politician's arsenal, are fast becoming a permanent fixture of the modern newsroom as well.

Development of the Modern Media Poll

Newspapers actually may have originated polling, albeit in a primitive form, with the straw polls they conducted to measure candidate strength in the 1800s. In 1824, for example, the *Harrisburg Pennsylvanian*, the *Raleigh Star*, and other newspapers used canvasses of political meetings "at which the sense of the people was taken" to report on the popular appeal of the presidential candidates.[1]

Other organizations eventually caught on to the interest in polling. In 1916 the *Literary Digest* asked its readers to send in information on public support in their communities for Woodrow Wilson and Charles Evans Hughes. Thereafter, the magazine mailed out straw ballots nationwide to names gleaned from automobile registration lists and telephone directories—until it was humiliated by its 1936 poll, which predicted that Alf Landon would defeat Franklin Roosevelt in a landslide.

In the mid-1930s the pioneers of more systematic, more scientific opinion polling were already involved with the media. Elmo Roper conducted preelection polls for *Fortune* magazine, Archibald Crossley did

1

polling for the Hearst chain, and George Gallup sold his findings to various subscribing newspapers. In the next several decades the connection between polling and the news media became close but not intimate. Poll reports by George Gallup and later by Louis Harris appeared as syndicated columns or news stories. Newspapers and eventually television networks hired individual pollsters or polling firms from time to time to conduct surveys or help oversee the analysis of election returns.

The first departure from this loose relationship between polls and the news media came in 1967 when CBS formed its own in-house polling operation. NBC and ABC also developed polling units. However, the birth of news media polling as we know it occurred in 1975 when the *New York Times* and CBS established a formal partnership to conduct polls. The *New York Times*, which was launching into uncharted waters, hoped to take advantage of the considerable statistical expertise at the CBS election and polling unit. CBS believed that an association with the *Times* might enhance its polls by lending more prominence and permanence to them. Both sides felt that it was important to establish some independence and distance from other polls, particularly those leaked by self-serving politicians or released by government agencies and various interest groups. The idea of designing questionnaires tailored to their specific news interests appealed to both the newspaper and the network. The partnership also would permit each to conduct many more polls and still control costs because they would split the expenses. And another benefit, not overlooked by either party but not publicly discussed, was that each might gain from advertising its name before the other's wide audience.

One outside development also helped foster the merger. Philip Meyer, then a national correspondent for Knight Newspapers, wrote *Precision Journalism,* which advocated that journalists incorporate more social science methods into their reporting. Beginning in 1974 he organized summer workshops where newspaper reporters were introduced to a variety of skills for analyzing data. The workshops produced disciples who returned to their newsrooms (including the *New York Times*) with Meyer's messianic message to lobby that it was both necessary and possible for their organizations to do their own polling.

Following the successful union of the *Times* and CBS, the idea of news media polls spread quickly. Many were also joint ventures, and several were spearheaded by participants from Meyer's seminar. The relationship between polls and the news media that developed after 1976 bore little resemblance to the hands-off pattern that had existed earlier. The two were now intimately tied together. A few polls, like the *New York Times/* CBS News poll, have become in-house operations—all the steps of polling, including interviewing respondents, are carried out by the sponsoring organizations. Other news organizations have contracted with commercial firms to conduct the actual interviewing (on an exclusive basis), and some have hired outside consultants to oversee their polls. These experts usually work closely with editors and reporters, who are often assigned to the public opinion beat. The editors and reporters help define the subjects of each poll, construct questionnaires, analyze results, and present findings. This process naturally requires much more time and money than simply taking poll information provided by an outside pollster and working it into news stories. But of course the most important difference between the pre- and post-1975 polls is that news organizations now devote considerably more column inches or more air time to coverage of their own polls (to which they attach the name of the network, station, newspaper, or magazine).

Today's news media polls vary widely in size, shape, and quality. Our favorite small, low-budget, local media poll—which also happens to anchor the goofy end of the spectrum—is one conducted every four years by radio station KEMB in Emmetsburg, Iowa. The station asks its listeners to flush their toilets when they hear the name of their favorite presidential candidate. It can then measure the support for each candidate because the water level at the local sewage treatment plant declines 1 inch for every 135 flushes. The station is proud of the forecasting accuracy of its poll, but concedes that there is some inadvertent voting. At the other end of the continuum is the *New York Times/*CBS News poll. The *New York Times* and CBS News polling operations employ sixty-five to seventy people, including a full-time staff of eight, several of whom are professionally trained. In 1988 the *Times* and CBS interviewed more than 80,000 respondents in thirty polls, at an estimated cost of nearly $1.5 million dollars.[2] Setting the KEMB poll from Emmetsburg against the *New York Times/*CBS News poll is of course comparing a rowboat to an ocean liner, but the two exemplify the differences in quality between polls conducted by news organizations in major metropolitan areas (which mostly poll national samples) and those conducted by local news outlets. These differences are far greater than the differences between the national media polls and academic surveys.

During the past twenty years, the significance of news media polls has skyrocketed. Everett Carll Ladd and John Benson document in chapter 2 the extraordinary growth in the number of news organizations that conduct polls. Perhaps just under half of daily newspapers, almost all large-circulation papers, and more than half of local TV stations now report on their own polls.[3] Accordingly, the number of polls has grown dramatically, and references to poll findings in newspapers and broadcasts have ballooned. News media polls now have eclipsed those from other sources, including polls conducted independently by commercial polling firms such as Gallup and Harris, academic surveys, and those conducted for interest groups, In short, the polls the American public knows about are now overwhelmingly news media polls.

If "to poll or not to poll" is not, then, the question facing most news organizations (as Ladd and Benson note, the forces propelling a greater use of polls worldwide seem inexorable), then what is? In our view, two questions need to be answered. First, what are the strengths and weaknesses of media polls—are there particular payoffs pollsters should be seeking and particular pitfalls they must avoid? Second, what is the impact of media polls on politics—are they a boon or a menace to democracy?

Strengths and Weaknesses

In conducting their own polls, news organizations help the political system in several ways. The most important benefit reflects the main reason why news organizations got into the polling business in the first place: by doing their own polls they can gain an additional check on the accountability of political and governmental leaders. Armed with their own polls, reporters need not blindly accept the claims of politicians who try to peddle their own polling information. An illustration of this occurred in a press briefing following the 1976 New Hampshire Democratic primary. Patrick Caddell, Jimmy Carter's pollster, told reporters that his analysis of the voting and survey data showed Carter had won by reassembling elements of the New Deal coalition, drawing from widely diverse segments of the Democratic primary electorate. However, one political reporter in the room, R.W. Apple of the *New York Times*, had studied the results of the first *New York Times*/CBS News exit poll and contradicted Caddell by noting that the media poll showed Carter had assembled a center-right coalition of moderate and conservative Democratic voters, not an across-the-board coalition.[4] This was a special moment in the continuing struggle between the watchdog press and political leaders.

The balance of power shifted permanently during that New Hampshire press briefing.

News media polls provide yet another source of accountability. Many years ago, V.O. Key pointed out that the principal role the public plays in American politics is to appraise the performance of elected officials by casting ballots to reward or punish their conduct in office.[5] Public opinion polls can provide additional readings of the public's evaluation of government performance between elections. News media polls have significantly augmented the handful of commercial polls that provided these between-election temperature charts, thus keeping those who govern more closely monitored. Some observers even complain that these frequent "votes of confidence" in the form of poll questions on performance inject too much accountability into the political system—they hamstring political leaders and make it hard to govern.

News media polls not only provide a check on the self-serving claims of government officials and candidates, but they also enable reporters to question some self-serving claims by small segments of the electorate. For example, in 1964 conservative allies of Senator Barry Goldwater insisted that there was hidden support for him, a "silent majority" just waiting to be heard. And one indicator of popular sentiment, letters to the editors of daily newspapers, suggested that the Goldwaterites were right. Letter writers favored Goldwater over Lyndon Johnson and felt that the federal government was too strong. However, this sentiment was not representative of public opinion at large, as polls at the time clearly showed.[6] On the other hand, reporters who dismissed Ronald Reagan as too right wing to attract a significant following, or ridiculed his statements as too foolish and simplistic to capture widespread support, should have consulted polling data. Polls can serve as a useful rein on our often imperfect intuitions.

Journalism in the United States usually reflects the prevailing sentiments and values of society, never straying too far from the public mood. Reporters also tend to imitate and reinforce their comrades. It is hardly surprising that, in a nation with a free, commercial, and highly competitive press, the climate of opinion would influence what messages the audience receives. Reporters consequently always need to question conventional wisdom, and polls can be a useful tool for doing this. They give reporters a way to test the riveting anecdote and dramatic personal experience that are the workhorses of traditional journalism. At the height of the Vietnam War, for example, polls showed that despite antiwar activity on many college campuses, conventional wisdom about young people was wrong. Most young people were hawkish on the war.

Critics of polls are fond of quoting Mark Twain's quip, "There are lies, damn lies, and statistics." In our view, statistician Frederick Mosteller has offered a wise reply: "It is easy to lie with statistics. But it is easier to lie without them."[7] If used properly, polls can strengthen a journalist's understanding and improve public enlightenment.

The obverse is that news media polls have potential harmful effects as well. Henry Brady and Gary Orren in chapter 4 suggest that the imperatives of survey research do not square easily with the imperatives of journalism, so that their union is inherently troubled. The ethos of survey research is one of methodological caution. Academic survey researchers are generally more worried about making a false assertion than missing a potentially important discovery. They subject their hypotheses to strict standards of proof and have no reluctance in attributing an event to random error or a complicated conjunction of causes. Academics are professional skeptics—slow, risk averse, and attentive to the weight of evidence.

Journalists work within a very different ethos. Their greatest concern is missing a major story or failing to go forward with a story, although it may turn out untrue. The need for speed and the demand for novel and interesting stories breeds an aggressive outlook that contrasts starkly with the more cautious statistical perspective. This clash of cultures poses special problems when polls are conducted and reported by the media.

Henry Brady and Gary Orren review three major sources of error in gathering and analyzing survey data: sampling error, measurement error, and specification error. The attention paid to these three sources of error by news organizations conducting polls and by the public reading or seeing stories based on polls is *inversely* related to their seriousness. For example, most media pollsters conscientiously report in their stories the "margin of error"—the probability-based range in which the sample results may diverge from the underlying population. Yet this focus on a single source of sampling error lends a false precision to polls and diverts attention from more serious threats to their validity. Properly defining the universe to be studied, achieving an acceptable response rate from those included in the sample, and reducing the bias resulting from troubling patterns of respondent selection and interview completion pose more formidable sampling problems.

But even these practical problems of sampling pale in significance compared with bad question wording or question order and defective underlying theories. Measurement error results when pollsters violate well-established precepts of questionnaire design, attempt to gauge opinions that do not really exist, and solicit responses based upon ill-formed and fleeting images. Specification error occurs when polls are designed and interpreted on the basis of inaccurate or inadequate conceptions of public opinion and political behavior (for example, theories about how issues influence voting, the role of race, and the dynamics of campaigns).

Brady and Orren recommend several ways to avoid the most serious pitfalls encountered in polling generally and the special problems of news media polling. These include investing more time in doing fewer surveys with better response rates, fewer topics and more questions on each topic, and more extensive and deeper analysis of results. Most of the recommendations thus address problems caused by the commanding importance of speed in the news business. Media pollsters need to slow down and think. "In polling, as on highways," Brady and Orren conclude, "speed kills."

What Brady and Orren see as a conflict between the needs of news organizations and the standards of survey research, Kathleen Frankovic in chapter 3 sees as a creative tension. The quest for better reporting of fast-breaking stories has led organizations to adapt existing survey research techniques and develop new ones. The need for a quick response and the availability of new technologies to provide it have presented news media pollsters with the challenge of balancing the desire for rapid—if not instantaneous—turnaround with the strictures of survey methodology.

Frankovic is not convinced that speed in polling is an inevitable cause of inaccuracy. Steps can be taken to minimize error associated with rapid turnaround, and the discipline of a tight time schedule can increase the quality and usefulness of a poll. She argues, in fact, that the trade-off between speed and quality made by media pollsters has been largely beneficial. For example, exit polls, an invention of news organizations, help reporters more accurately forecast election outcomes, plan their coverage and, most important, interpret the meaning of elections—all in a very short time. They have become such a prominent feature of election reporting that it is hard to imagine how the networks and newspapers could do their jobs without them.

Yet exit polls are conducted under conditions that impose severe limitations on the collection and analysis of survey responses. Errors can result from poorly designed samples, misestimates of turnout in sample precincts, high rates of refusal to participate that vary across groups of voters, or inadequately constructed questionnaires. Bad questionnaires are particularly troublesome given the requirement that exit polls be self-administered and brief enough to be completed within a few minutes. One important way of coping with these potential errors—examining responses across several exit polls—has been lost with the pooling of network exit polling resources into a single consortium.

Advances in computing have facilitated rapid processing of enormous amounts of survey data. News organizations have exploited these developments by conducting more and more instant polls to gauge public reactions to events and crises, tracking polls to measure daily fluctuations in support for candidates, and panel surveys to study opinion change at the individual level. Each method serves the needs of news organizations for timely readings of public opinion, but each is prey to serious errors that may well distort the true opinion being measured. Instant polls and overnight tracking polls, for example, not only present severe methodological problems—the difficulty of reaching sample respondents who are not at home or respondents not available on the first try—but they also introduce problems of substantive interpretation. As Albert Cantril has noted, the combination of tracking polls and journalistic competition for news has had "the effect of quickening the cycle within which the significance of an event is assessed." However, often "the political metabolism of the general public operates on a different time clock" than the blitzkrieg requirements of the tracking or instant polls. After an event, opinion may take awhile to settle.[8]

A host of problems for media polls can be traced to competitive pressures of the marketplace. Frankovic warns that shrinking news budgets and the need to control costs at the television networks may lead to a greater reliance on call-in "polls" using 800 or 900 telephone numbers. These call-ins, which vaguely resemble valid scientific polls, pollute the survey process. The networks' main interest in them is not measuring public opinion but getting the audience involved in what is on the screen. Eventually, call-ins may use cost-cutting devices that ask prerecorded questions and record peoples' answers via telephone technology. All in all, financial pressures may lead the networks in the same direction as

Ross Perot's electronic town meetings, with audience involvement taking precedence over the accurate measurement of peoples' attitudes.

Although news organizations make heavy use of polls conducted by others, once a newspaper or television station invests seriously in polling, it is likely to give its own surveys top billing, regardless of the significance of the results. The news organization has a vested interest in showcasing its poll and trumpeting the results. "Polls aren't news," said former NBC reporter Ken Bode. "They only exist because we paid for them. If they were so good and were really newsworthy, why didn't everybody else report them? I believe they are a form of corporate advertising." Paul Taylor of the *Washington Post* echoes these sentiments in frankly admitting a news organization's interest in its own poll: "there is institutional pressure. You spend a lot of money on polls."[9] It is not surprising, then, that news organizations often publish results that political pollsters or academic survey researchers take with a good deal of salt—because the opinion is unstable, volatile, or premature.

Not only do financial pressures drive news organizations to promote their own poll results, but personal and institutional pride sometimes leads them to push their polls too hard. News organizations have been known to publish incomplete or stale results simply to beat a competitor to the punch and make a splash in the first edition.

Some consequences of the intense competition, which on first blush seem harmful, may in fact be beneficial. The proliferation of polls has produced contradictory results from one poll to the next that baffle the public and damage the credibility of polling. In the early summer of 1992, national news organizations reported divergent poll findings for independent presidential candidate Ross Perot's standing in the race. Some had him leading a three-way race with George Bush and Bill Clinton. Others consigned him to second place. Immediate public reaction was to blame the polls for inaccurate and unreliable findings. But more sober reflection produced a less damning interpretation. Not only was Perot's standing at that early stage of the campaign based on fragmentary knowledge and fleeting impressions, subject to sudden shifts as people learned more about him, but the measurement of his support was also more susceptible than normal to variations across polls in question wording and question order.

Michael Kagay in chapter 5 explores the sources of variability in poll findings. Discrepant or even contradictory results, he argues, are due less to shoddy, error-prone methods than to the competitive instincts of news organizations. The business leads competing polls to chase the same hot stories, but competitive forces also lead each organization to conduct its poll with its own distinctive approach to question wording, analysis, interpretation, and presentation of results. No-fault variability necessarily follows.

Kagay investigates why well-designed polls have produced discrepant findings on the standing of presidential candidates, the war in the Persian Gulf, and abortion. Variability in presidential trial heats is often due to the timing of polls (those taken before, during, and just after the party conventions can give a temporary and unrealistic picture of the candidates' underlying strength); the stage of the campaign (the earlier polls are conducted, the more uncrystallized opinions will produce unstable results); and the placement of questions (some pollsters seek to simulate campaign learning by asking questions about certain issues or candidate traits before posing the trial heat). Variability may also stem from the population sampled (at different times and for different reasons, pollsters target all adults, registered voters, and likely voters) and the presentation of results (especially the allocation of undecided voters). Polls on foreign policy are particularly sensitive to dramatic events, appeals from leaders, and the presentation of policy options. And surveys of complex domestic issues (such as abortion) can cause confusion by tapping different values and triggering seemingly contradictory opinions.

But the availability of numerous polls on the same subject also gives the close observer an opportunity to detect the effects of variation in method, discount idiosyncratic polls more quickly, and develop a richer, more nuanced view of public opinion. Careful reporting of survey methods and potential sources of variability, combined with a focus on the overall pattern of results from a series of polls, can therefore make the proliferation of polls and the competition among them a virtue rather than a liability. The costs of redundancy in polling stories thus are low while the benefits of a competitive, pluralistic press scrambling to find out what the public thinks are high. Truth usually lies in the preponderance of evidence from a multiplicity of polls using divergent approaches.

Unfortunately, recent financial straits at the networks have led them to consolidate exit polling. Since 1990 ABC, CBS, CNN, and NBC have combined their resources into a single polling consortium, Voter Research & Surveys, to conduct exit polls. The reduction from three exit polls to one eliminates the possibility of the cross-checking Kagay discusses.

News media polls focus on elections, and the horse race among candidates in particular, an impression confirmed by Ladd and Benson. But the who's up, who's down character of election coverage began long before public opinion polls became prevalent. It probably is fair to assume, however, that the heavy stream of news media polls during campaigns—and the fact that most news organizations have their own supply of polls close at hand—has reinforced the tendency for coverage to concentrate on candidate standings. There is no necessary reason for this. News media polls could be used to explore the public's view on the important issues of the day. For the most part, however, this has not happened. The almost daily fare of horse race numbers frames the public dialogue, including news reports and commentary, and colors the media's interpretation.

Speaking of horse race and issue polling, there is a contrast between the leverage and independence that polls afford news organizations vis à vis political candidates and the leverage they afford vis à vis interest groups. The news media acquired substantial protection against the self-serving claims of politicians when they started conducting their own polls. However, the limited attention given to policy issues in election year surveys and the limited number of serious issue polls conducted by news pollsters leaves the press with far less protection against the claims of public and private interest groups. This greater vulnerability is demonstrated whenever an interest group sponsors a poll on health issues, the environment, education, or crime, and news organizations must contact an academic expert who can be an impartial judge to assess the poll and decide whether it is trustworthy.

Although media polls simply reinforce the long-existing tendency for horse race stories to dominate election coverage, they may have helped introduce something new into election coverage—the flurry of strategy and tactics stories. It is this kind of news coverage that has grown the most since 1976.[10] In strategy and tactics stories, reporters try to reveal what a campaign is really focusing on, evaluating its inner workings. The surge of this inside reporting has undoubtedly been fueled by the newsroom's access to polls. Armed with large sample polls, tracking polls, and focus-group data, reporters are well equipped to play the game along with the campaign operatives.

A familiar complaint about media polls is that they have displaced traditional newsgathering methods—shoe leather journalism. We do not know whether the arrival of polls has caused this change, but the fascination with polls probably has changed how reporters perceive the world.

Political scientist Thomas Patterson has found that when a candidate is doing well in horse race polls, he or she is portrayed by the press as strong, intelligent, thoughtful, and capable. When the candidate is languishing, he or she is characterized as weak, stiff, hesitant, and incompetent.[11]

In a similar vein, Bill Kovach, former editor of the *Atlanta-Journal Constitution* and Washington bureau chief of the *New York Times,* has suggested that press preoccupation with opinion has crowded out an appreciation for objective fact. Instead of reporting that people think banks are redlining ghetto residents, reporters should use objective information to report that indeed the banks are doing so.[12]

Boon or Menace?

What is the impact of news media polls? Are they a help or a hindrance to the political process, a boon or a menace?

How do polls influence the public? Critics argue that frequent reporting of candidate standings conditions the electorate to evaluate candidates on grounds of electability and diminishes attention to more substantive matters. They also worry that the dissemination of poll results can directly affect the choice of candidates by voters, either through a bandwagon effect (drawing additional supporters to the candidate who is far ahead) or an underdog effect (sending sympathetic voters to a weaker opponent). Finally, critics often express concern that preelection polls and election night projections showing one candidate far ahead have a depressing effect on turnout.

After carefully reviewing the evidence and noting the shortcomings of most studies designed to demonstrate conclusively the direct effects of poll results on the public, Michael Traugott concludes that media polls do matter, but in modest, contingent, and often offsetting ways (chapter 6). Voters are most likely to be influenced by polls when other cues are not readily available (as in early primary elections) and when evidence of viability in multicandidate contests is needed by voters to avoid wasting their votes. Poll standings are critical to third party or independent presidential candidates, whose support in preelection trial heats shapes whether they are viewed as serious contenders or spoilers.

During the late spring of 1992 Ross Perot's independent bid for the presidency was legitimized and given momentum by his strong showing in exit polls of Democratic and Republican state primary elections. In this case the succession of poll encounters among George Bush, Bill Clinton, and Perot overwhelmed the primary results and became a surrogate presidential selection process. Just how many citizens' views of the Perot candidacy were shaped by the poll results is unknown. But no one disputes the significance of the indirect effects: the enthusiasm of volunteers, the receptiveness of politically active people, the quantity and character of news coverage.

These indirect effects on the public are probably larger and more consequential than direct effects, but also more problematic. Thus the polls must be carefully constructed and the results reported responsibly. Polls can influence public opinion as well as measure it. News organizations have an obligation to use them in a way that facilitates the discussion between citizens and their leaders, not intrude upon it in an unnecessary and unwarranted fashion.

How well are the media meeting that obligation? Are polls the servant of journalism and democracy or an impediment? In chapter 7 E.J. Dionne, Jr., concedes that much of the criticism of the increasing use of polls by reporters has merit. At root is the elevation of technique over substance. Contemporary political reporting has put a premium on the inside story of presidential campaigns and has given short shrift to the views and intentions of the candidates and their prospects for governing successfully. An obsession with polls threatens to divert journalism from helping citizens make informed decisions and encouraging a wide-ranging democratic debate.

The damaging effects of media polls are most visible in the frenzy of reporters demanding that candidates react to the latest published results of the horse race. From the infamous fifty-state poll released by ABC News on the eve of the second 1988 presidential debate between George Bush and Michael Dukakis to the daily tracking polls leading up to the 1992 New Hampshire primary, news surveys often distort the coverage of campaigns by reporters and demean the role of citizens as the subjects of democratic politics.

Yet Dionne reminds us that the obsession with polls by media organizations is more symptom than cause of the denigration of democratic debate in contemporary political campaigns. The decline in the importance of political parties has foisted upon the media responsibility for vetting presidential candidates and deciding who among them should be taken seriously. Polls offer journalists a seemingly objective, apolitical way of meeting that responsibility. Similarly, the absence of a clear agenda that would focus the discussion between candidates and voters on important matters elevates polls—and the accompanying emphasis on strategy and tactics—to a more prominent position in campaign coverage.

The challenge is to use the polls not as substitutes for the thinking, reporting, and analyzing that are the hallmarks of journalism, but rather as a means of exploding the stereotypes of reporters and contesting the interpretations of self-interested players. Dionne offers numerous examples from the 1980, 1984, 1988, and 1992 presidential campaigns in which journalists effectively used polls to better answer questions they would have asked even if polls had not existed. He tenders two rules for media polling: "First, polls are most valuable in challenging and overturning preconceptions; second, polls should be used to describe the complexity of public opinion, not oversimplify what citizens think."

The careless use of polls by journalists can exacerbate some of the worst tendencies of American democracy, especially the disingenuousness of its leaders and the passivity of its citizens. Properly used, polls can help citizens come to a better-informed and more enlightened judgment about the public agenda.

Recommendations

The debate over the impact of media polls is properly part of a larger discussion of the effectiveness of American political institutions. It is by now a commonplace to note the widespread public dissatisfaction with government and with the politicians elected to run it. Although this distemper may well be rooted in the mediocre performance of the economy over the past two decades and in the unpleasant choices forced by high budget deficits and a restructuring of the global economy, the political system has probably made matters worse.

Especially frustrating has been the growing separation between campaigning and governing. Increasingly, elections seem divorced from the serious problems that confront government and the policy options from which it must choose. Citizens see little connection between what politicians say during campaigns and what they do in office. Politicians view elections as distasteful encounters to survive rather than as opportunities to build a popular mandate for public action. Instead of forming and empowering a government, campaigns and elections too often divide and enfeeble it.

The process seems to encourage a fundamentally dishonest conversation between leaders and citizens. Leaders are reluctant to confront their constituents with sober facts and difficult choices. They content themselves with servicing public preferences while ignoring public needs. The public clings to incompatible policy goals and deadlock-prone political arrangements and then strikes out at the political system for its failure to take decisive action to deal with the country's problems. Each gets more and more frustrated and angry with the other, but little effort is made to initiate a constructive process of debate and deliberation.

A mechanistic use of polls and a static view of public opinion work to reinforce the risk-averse, escapist character of American politics. A more enlightened approach to polling and an appreciation of the possibilities of public persuasion offer some hope of breaking that pattern. It is in this context, therefore, that we offer a number of suggestions for improving the way polls are conducted and reported by news organizations.

—The proliferation of news organizations that conduct polls makes it possible and reasonable for individual organizations to concentrate polling resources on depth rather than breadth. This means fewer polls of higher quality: larger samples, more callbacks, multiple questions to measure attitudes on a more limited number of topics, screens to ensure that a topic is important to respondents and that they have an opinion about it, experiments with item wording and question order, and adequate time and space for analysis and interpretation. It also means less emphasis on the horse race and more on underlying attitudes and opinions on issues.

—Polls designed to gauge public reactions to events or crises are especially prone to error because of the need for interviews to be completed rapidly. Special care should be taken to discern possible sources of bias in these "instant polls" and to discount the findings when reported to the public. These polls are the most expendable.

—In no case should 800 or 900 call-in audience participation activities be labeled polls or surveys and thereby given scientific respectability. Serious efforts through town meetings and call-in shows to involve citizens in discussions about the public agenda are commendable, but the same cannot be said for associated measurements of public opinion. From CBS's "America on the Line" to Ross Perot's "electronic town meetings," call-in surveys are prone to serious distortion from self-selection and manipulation of opinion by politicians or interest groups.

—Media polls should become a routine tool of political reporting, used in conjunction with other information sources. Poll results should assist in reporting a story, not become the subject of the story. Horse race results should be downplayed, and where appropriate relegated to a box on the inside pages. Findings from other polls, aggregate data, historical patterns, and intensive interviews with citizens should be used to interpret poll results and put them in context. Focus groups should not become an inexpensive method of survey research; they should be conducted in association with polls.

—Media organizations should resist efforts to dramatize and concretize what are fragile, unformed opinions and unstable, event-driven findings. This requires special attention to the meaning and utility of measures of voter preference for candidates at different stages of the campaign. It also means that pollsters should be sensitive to the saliency of topics for the people they are surveying, including respondents' levels of interest and knowledge and the stability of their responses over time.

—News media polls are egregiously underanalyzed, and more resources should be invested in their analysis and interpretation. Media pollsters (especially at the regional and local levels) should familiarize themselves with theories of opinion formation and methods of multivariate analysis.

—Fuller disclosures of sampling information and survey methods is desirable, as is a more honest discussion of the several sources of error to which polls are prey. If the polling story devotes substantial attention to a subgroup, then the sampling error for that subgroup should be reported. This also includes disclosure of response rates. Polling professionals should closely examine the response rate problem, and try to agree on a minimum standard of response rate for publication.

We offer these recommendations in full recognition that some national media organizations have already incorporated many of them into their polling operations. Improvements in quality and innovative solutions to special news needs have been hallmarks of media polling in the past two decades. But the overall record at national, regional, and local levels is sufficiently spotty and the problems posed by the proliferation of polls sufficiently worrisome for American democracy that attention to these suggestions is merited.

Conclusion

Few changes have transformed American politics more in the past two decades than the avalanche of news media polls. To appreciate the dimensions of this transformation, imagine how different our politics would be if there were no news media polls today. What began two decades ago as a modest effort to increase the independence and quality of reporting on elections has become a dominant, obtrusive feature of news coverage. Polls are a staple of contemporary journalism, a reporting tool embraced by broadcast and print media at the national and local levels. At its best, polling serves the noble purpose identified by George Gallup as monitoring the pulse of democracy, letting the people set the public agenda. Yet the proliferation of polls conducted and reported by news organizations threatens at times to undermine the discussion between citizens and leaders that is at the very core of American democracy.

This book is designed to take stock of this crucial development in political reporting and to weigh its impact. We believe that media polls have an important place in American public life but that it is essential they be put in their place. Polls should help report news, not create it. They should facilitate the work of political reporters, not substitute for it. Polls should clarify and evaluate the messages of candidates, not drown them out. They should provide a reality check on political operatives and pundits, not elevate their obsession with strategy and tactics to the lead story of the campaign. Finally, polls should convey to citizens and leaders the complex nature of public opinion and the limits and possibilities of deliberation and persuasion.

Media polls can be a boon or a menace to democracy. They can help enrich news reporting, educate citizens, and hold political leaders more accountable. On balance, however, most news media polls have not yet realized their greatest potential. It is time to make the necessary corrections.

Notes

1. Charles W. Roll, Jr., and Albert H. Cantril, *Polls: Their Use and Misuse in Politics* (Basic Books, 1972), pp. 7–8.

2. Interviews with Michael Kagay, *New York Times,* and Kathleen Frankovic, CBS News.

3. Jack K. Holley, "The Press and Political Polling," in Paul J. Lavrakas and Jack K. Holley, eds., *Polling and Presidential Election Coverage* (Newbury Park, Calif.: Sage Publications, 1991), pp. 225–27, 235–36; and Everett Carll Ladd and John Benson, chapter 2 in this volume.

4. The findings in the *New York Times*/CBS News Poll made good sense since Carter faced a field of liberal opponents: Morris Udall, Birch Bayh, Sargent Shriver, and Fred Harris. More conservative candidates Henry Jackson and George Wallace had decided not to compete in the New Hampshire primary.

5. V. O. Key, Jr., *The Responsible Electorate: Rationality in Presidential Voting, 1936–1960* (Harvard University Press, 1966).

6. Philip E. Converse, Aage R. Clausen, and Warren E. Miller, "Electoral Myth and Reality: The 1964 Election," *American Political Science Review*, vol. 59 (June 1965), pp. 321–36.

7. Interview with Frederick Mosteller.

8. Albert H. Cantril, *The Opinion Connection: Polling, Politics, and the Press* (Washington: CQ Press, 1991), p. 70.

9. Bode and Taylor are quoted in Cantril, *The Opinion Connection*, pp. 66–67.

10. Gary Orren, "Blurring the Lines: Candidates and Reporters in American Elections," Harvard University, 1992.

11. Thomas Patterson, "News Images: Journalists' Portrayals of Candidates," Syracuse University, 1992.

12. Bill Kovach, "Too Much Opinion, at the Expense of Fact," *New York Times*, September 13, 1989, p. A31.

Chapter 2

The Growth of News Polls in American Politics

EVERETT CARLL LADD AND JOHN BENSON

N EWS ORGANIZATIONS began to use opinion polling based on systematic sampling in the 1930s. Gallup polls, supported at least in part through newspaper syndication, and Roper polls, conducted on a continuing basis for *Fortune* magazine, were pathbreaking enterprises of estimable quality. Not until the late 1960s, however, did a news organization conduct its own polls. In 1967 CBS News established the precursor of its Election and Survey Unit under the direction of Warren Mitofsky and not only supported the enterprise but used its own staff to perform all polling activities. CBS used exit polling in combination with precinct returns in the 1967 Kentucky gubernatorial race and again in the 1968 presidential primaries. In 1972 it conducted a nationwide exit poll for analysis only.[1] The network entered into a polling partnership with the *New York Times* in 1975, an association that continues.

The roster of national news media assuming direct responsibility for conducting opinion and election polls—lending their names and standing to the enterprises, determining what is asked and when, and providing major if not exclusive financial sponsorship—has grown substantially in the past two decades, as has the number of polls. Just two major organizations conducted 3 separate polls in the 1972 election year, but seven conducted 122 in 1980, and eight conducted 259 in 1988, according to the Roper Center's 1989 survey of news media polling (see appendix).

We thank Marianne Simonoff, research assistant at the Roper Center, and Lynn A. Zayachkiwsky, administrative assistant to the executive director of the Roper Center, for their contributions to this study.

And some of those that counted as single surveys—the exit polls on election day—were in fact large, complex amalgams of independent state surveys and a national poll. In 1988 Gallup expanded its pre-primary and general election polling for CONUS Communications (CONUS included 24 member TV stations and 110 newspapers that were given exclusive rights to the polls in their local markets). And from Labor Day until the election, KRC Communications, in cooperation with the American Political Network, released daily results tracking the presidential race.[2] APN's Presidential Hotline provided subscribers access to daily summaries containing abstracts of political stories carried by news media, interviews with campaign insiders, and highlights of congressional races. Hotline's daily poll update and fifty-state report summarized major findings from national, state, and local surveys. Because no news organization could otherwise cover polling in all races, Hotline became an enormously useful resource, greatly extending access.

In 1990 CBS, NBC, ABC, and CNN joined ranks, largely for financial reasons, to create a single organization to do all their exit polling (but not other forms of survey research). Known as Voter Research & Surveys (VRS), the consortium was the only major organization engaged in exit polling during the 1990 primary and general elections. Whether this sharp contraction in the number of separate election day polling operations will become permanent or whether other organizations will also engage in polling is not clear. VRS had fifty-eight television and newspaper subscribers in 1990 and expects to have many more in 1992.

Although election years, especially presidential election years, show heavier media polling than do off years, the major news organizations are now active in all seasons, and the growth of off-year polling parallels that found in election years. In 1985 the major organizations conducted 73 surveys; in 1989 they conducted 161. All forms of polling have been sharply on the rise, a growth well documented by the number of questions. In the 1960s some 6,900 questions were asked; in the 1970s the total was 37,000, and in the 1980s about 89,000. The recent surge of polling by the major national media is especially striking. Since the mid-1970s the number of questions posed in national surveys by the major organizations has increased dramatically—from 1,412 in 1976, to 3,390 in 1980, to 4,458 in 1984, and 4,666 in 1988. In years immediately following presidential elections the totals have also risen strongly, from 643 in 1977 to 3,912 in 1989 (figure 2-1). And 800 more questions were posed

Figure 2-1. *Number of Poll Questions Asked by Selected Major News Organizations, 1970–90* [a]

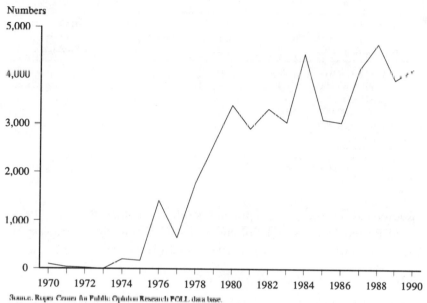

Source. Roper Center for Public Opinion Research POLL data base.

a. See appendix for news organizations included. Questions are from nationwide surveys only and exclude those on demographic variables. Some questions may have been missed, but the POLL data base is generally complete, and omissions should not affect results portrayed.

by the major media polls in 1990, an off year with congressional elections, than in 1982, the comparable year with the previous high number.

The Roper Center Survey

Although the polls of the major news organizations get the most attention because of their sponsors' newsgathering resources and large audiences, this work is only a more visible part of the growing sponsorship of polling by newspapers with state and regional coverage and by local television stations. It was to chart this growth more precisely that the Roper Center conducted the media survey in 1989. The sample consisted of three groups (for full details see the appendix): 13 print and video news organizations that alone or in concert were defined as major pollsters; 100 newspapers (excluding 5 appearing among the major pollsters) that had circulations of 115,000 or more; and 54 commercial VHF television stations. The following discussion is based on the results of this survey. The

Table 2-1.   *Newspapers Engaged in News Polling, by Circulation,*
Survey Results, 1978–90
Percent

Circulation	Rippey (1978)	Demers (1986)	Holley-Northwestern[a] (1989)	Roper Center[b] (1989–90)
10,000 or fewer	22	18 ⎫	35	. . .
10,001– 25,000	34	29 ⎭		. . .
25,001– 50,000	43	41	54	. . .
50,001–100,000	60	58	52	. . .
100,001–250,000	71	76	83 ⎫	82
250,001 or more	77	86	87 ⎭	

Sources: See text note 3 and Roper Center survey of news media polling described in appendix.
a. Question specified political polling.
b. Question specified "for news purposes."

discussion also refers to three previous studies—by John Rippey in 1978, David Pearce Demers in 1986, and Jack Holley and the Northwestern University Survey Laboratory in 1989—that used similar samples.[3]

Incidence of Media Polling

The survey found that 82 percent of large-circulation newspapers and 56 percent of TV stations were substantially involved in news polling. TV stations are less involved, in part because many can rely on their networks' polling on national matters. Our findings on newspaper polling were consistent with those in the 1989 Holley-Northwestern survey (table 2-1). As for the longer-term incidence of polling, in 1986 Demers concluded that it rose sharply at daily newspapers during the 1960s and early 1970s, but he found no significant change from 1978 to 1986.[4] Rippey found 37 percent of all daily newspapers engaged in polling in 1978, Demers found 35 percent in 1986, and Holley reported 40 percent in 1989. If only newspapers of 100,000 or more circulation are considered, there has been a slight increase (table 2-1). Of course, once 75 percent of the big newspapers had become involved in polling, it was inevitable that further growth would be slow: the remaining nonpolling papers include those too financially strapped to participate and a few that are philosophically opposed.

Even though the percentage of newspapers substantially involved in news-related polling has increased only slightly in the past decade, the frequency of their surveys more than doubled between 1976 and 1988. Among TV stations, the mean number nearly tripled (table 2-2). Some

Table 2-2.   *Mean Number of Media Polls Conducted Annually,*
by Media Type, Selected Years, 1968–89

Year	Newspapers	Television stations	Major media organizations[a]
1968	1.7	0	0
1972	2.0	0.3	0.4
1976	2.1	2.2	4.4
1980	3.2	5.6	16.4
1984	3.9	6.2	26.6
1988	5.6	6.1	32.4
1989	5.2	7.1	20.1

Source: Roper Center 1989 survey.
a. See appendix for definition.

caution needs to be applied to such figures, however, because institutional memory tends to be weak at many news organizations—when asked how many surveys his organization had conducted in 1968, one respondent wrote that the period was "prehistory." Nonetheless, the growth appears substantial, if not quite matching that among the major national news organizations.

The Focus of Polling

Election coverage is obviously a driving force behind the news media's use of polling. Eighty-seven percent of newspapers and 94 percent of TV stations that completed our questionnaire reported having engaged in election polling during 1988-89. Exit polls, a prominent subgenre of election polls, were used by 69 percent of TV stations in 1988 but only 15 percent of newspapers. The survey did not explore the reasons, but television's unquenchable thirst for live election night reporting is probably the major factor.

Demers expressed concern that polling coverage had drifted from trying to gauge the public's views on issues to trying to see who was leading— so-called horse race polling. Newspapers were, he found, more likely in 1986 than they had been in 1978 to poll on primary elections (53 percent to 38 percent) and referendums (46 percent to 35 percent) than to poll on pending legislation (35 percent to 48 percent). Our findings do not permit us to assess this matter; they only confirm that elections are indeed a significant concern of media polling. Not, however, an overwhelming concern. Newspapers devoted about 40 percent and TV stations 60 percent of their recent survey activity to election inquiries. Nearly 60 percent of the questions asked in the 1980, 1984, and 1988 presidential years by

Table 2-3.   *Distribution of Topics in Media Polls, by Type of Media, 1989*
Percent

Topic	Newspapers	TV stations	Major organizations[a]
Local issues and policy	32	44	11
Statewide issues and policy	43	44	8
National or international issues and policy	15	11	62
Subjects of personal rather than political interest	11	2	19

Source: Roper Center survey of news media polling.
a. See appendix for definition.

major news organizations also concerned horse races, broadly construed. But citing only election year data is stacking the deck. Just 30 percent of the questions from these organizations in the four years from August 1987 through August 1991 were of the horse race variety.

There are significant distinctions in the focus of newspaper and television surveys. Eighty-one percent of both groups reported using polls to measure public preferences on statewide issues. But newspapers had a higher involvement with polling on national and international issues (64 percent to 50 percent), although only one of the papers actually conducts nationwide polls. TV stations were more likely to poll on local issues. As for the frequency with which the various media focus on certain topics, TV stations devote equal polling attention to local and statewide issues. Newspapers devote less to local issues, more to national and international matters (table 2-3). Newspapers were also much more likely to poll to measure responses on personal rather than political subjects. The major national news organizations and the syndicated services, as expected, supplied most of the polling on national and international affairs.

Newspapers and TV stations are remarkably similar in the geographic reach of their polling. The percentage of polling devoted to a statewide area was 51 percent for newspapers (excluding the national organizations) and 59 percent for TV stations. Polling devoted to a city, county, or local area was 46 percent for papers, 41 percent for television. Almost no nationwide polling was conducted by either group because both rely on the major national news organizations (who devote nearly 70 percent of their polling to nationwide surveys) and syndicated services such as the Gallup poll, the Harris surveys, and CONUS Communications.

A study of 122 *Chicago Tribune* stories that relied on polling (see chapter 4) helps illuminate the interaction between an individual newspaper, the major national news organizations, and the syndicated services. Between July 1, 1988, and December 31, 1989, the *Tribune* itself sponsored polls mentioned in 23 of 29 stories (79 percent) written about the state or a local area and citing media surveys. Only 5 of 28 stories written about national issues and citing media surveys relied on *Tribune*-sponsored polls. Seventeen national stories (61 percent) relied on surveys by major news organizations, 5 more (18 percent) on syndicated Gallup and Harris surveys, and 3 others (11 percent) on miscellaneous other media surveys.[5]

Reaching Respondents

One of the most striking findings of our survey was that not a single newspaper or TV station in our sample relied entirely on personal interviews, and only a few used a mix of telephone and personal methods. Telephone surveys were, of course, already dominant in 1978 when Rippey reported that 25 percent of all newspapers said they always used phones, 32 percent used them most often, and 13 percent used them occasionally. None said they never polled by telephone. But the personal interviewing that still held the fort in 1978 has now been overwhelmed by some combination of telephone polling's relative inexpensiveness, its convenience, and quality assessment factors.

Organizational Structure of Polling

Both newspapers and TV stations in our survey said they relied more heavily on outside survey firms for polling than on in-house staff and facilities. This reliance has presumably followed the expanded polling by Gallup for CONUS in 1988 and the activities of the American Political Network. Among newspapers, 20 percent used in-house staff and facilities, 46 percent contracted out, and 25 percent used a mix of the two. Among TV stations, 18 percent relied on in-house facilities, 64 percent contracted out, and 24 percent employed a mix. The Holley-Northwestern survey also reported a greater use of outside than of in-house arrangements among newspapers of 100,000 or more circulation. Demers found that use of outside consultants for framing questions, conducting interviews, and analyzing results doubled between 1978 and 1986. All these findings

support his thesis that newspaper polling became increasingly profes-
sionalized in the late 1970s and 1980s as papers relied less on their own
news staffs and more on outside commercial or academic polling organizations.[6]

To understand further the workings of media polling arrangements,
we asked which staff member in each organization headed news-related
polling and to whom he or she reported. Among newspapers the person
most likely to be responsible for polling was the state or metropolitan
editor (21 percent), the research manager (19 percent), the marketing
services editor (13 percent), or the assistant managing editor (13 percent).
As one newspaper respondent said, "No particular person [heads up our
news-related polling]. Whichever editor has the idea or related story is
in charge." Another claimed, "There's no real organization. One of us
will come up with the idea for a survey . . . and talk to the marketing
and circulation people." Among TV stations the head of news-related
polling was almost always the news director or the assistant news director.
Even on the next level up, the authority was relatively diffuse at newspapers. The heads of news-related polling reported to their managing
editors or assistant managing editors on 51 percent of the papers; others
reported to the editor or executive editor (24 percent) or the city editor
(11 percent). Only two people hold authority in TV stations, the general
manager and the news director.

How Newspapers Use Polling

The investigation of the *Chicago Tribune*'s poll-related stories, reported in chapter 4 found that half relied on media surveys, and half of
those were sponsored by the *Tribune*. Nonmedia polls were the basis for
a little less than half of the stories (table 2-4). Nonmedia polls fit into a
potpourri of categories. Only 4 percent of the *Tribune* articles mentioned
polls conducted for candidates or parties, perhaps because the kinds of
concerns about accuracy that Brady and Gary Orren express in a later
chapter in this volume are especially important for this category. But
these polls are often important parts of the dynamics of political campaigns. For example, on January 13, 1989, the *Tribune* reported that a
poll done for Mayor Sawyer's opponent Richard Daley showed "Sawyer
Closing Gap on Daley." A report on a February 15 poll was headlined
"Sawyer Poll Shows Tight Race."

A more important category for the *Tribune* included polls done for

Table 2-4. Chicago Tribune *Stories Based on Media and Nonmedia Surveys, July 1, 1988–December 31, 1989*

Type of poll	Number of stories	Percent of stories	Number involving an election	Percent
News media polls	60	49	36	60
National media	19	16	9	47
Tribune-sponsored	28	23	23	82
Other local media	4	3	3	75
Gallup and Harris syndicated	6	5	1	17
Miscellaneous	3	3	0	0
Nonmedia polls	55	45	14	25
Candidate or party	5	4	n.a.	n.a.
Education or research	13	11	n.a.	n.a.
Government or corporation	16	13	n.a.	n.a.
Polling firm	9	7	n.a.	n.a.
Lobbying	12	10	n.a.	n.a.
Unknown	7	6	4	53

Source: Henry Brady.
n.a. Not available.

(and usually by) educational and research organizations. Their topics are particularly varied; in the *Tribune* articles, for example, there were polls on Mexican migration to the United States, the threat of communism, and the impact of joblessness on one-parent families. Two ongoing series are often cited by the national news media. The General Social Survey, done annually by the National Opinion Research Center at the University of Chicago, is an authoritative source on trends in social attitudes and behavior. The National Election Studies, done by the Center for Political Studies at the University of Michigan every two years, is a helpful window on electoral behavior. These are, however, surveys conducted for research purposes; although their findings occasionally provide news, the intended consumers are sociologists and political scientists. Neither series was cited in the *Tribune*, but other surveys conducted at both Michigan and Chicago were mentioned.

The surveys cited in the remaining stories varied in topics covered and purposes. About 13 percent were conducted for government agencies or corporations, 10 percent for lobbying groups. A firm other than Gallup, Harris, or Roper did 7 percent, but the client was not identified. Many of the studies conducted for government, corporations, or lobbyists are done by these kinds of polling firms and involve established researchers.

They often provide data on public opinion for the express purpose of devising strategies to influence it.

About half of the stories based on surveys by the major national news organizations and more than three-quarters of the stories using *Tribune*-sponsored polls had to do with an election (table 2-4). Altogether 60 percent of stories based on media polls concerned elections, as opposed to only 29 percent of stories based on other kinds of surveys.

Once a newspaper such as the *Tribune* decides to invest in polling, it is likely to discuss the results prominently. For example, 82 percent of the articles mentioning *Tribune*-sponsored polls appeared on the front page of the newspaper. Only 28 percent mentioning other media surveys and 18 percent mentioning nonmedia surveys were so featured.

The *New York Times* was also a heavy user of its own surveys. It conducted 126 polls alone or in conjunction with CBS News during the past four presidential election years and ran 697 stories based on them, an average of 5.5 stories per survey. Thirty percent ran on the front page.[7]

Implications

The growth of media polling has been enormous and steady. Each year has seen more polls than its comparable predecessor—1988 more than the preceding presidential year, 1989 more than 1985, and so forth. Though budgetary limits and sheer saturation may well slow the growth in the future, as economic constraints slowed exit polling in 1990, growth will not stop.

News media are led by their varied positions and interests to use polls in differing fashions. Local television stations employ exit polls more often than local newspapers; the state and metropolitan press poll on national issues less often than the major national news media. But the old distinction between horse race polling and issues polling—finding out what the people really think about the big decisions before them—is irrelevant. News media do a lot of both. There seems to be no empirical basis for saying that one form crowds out the other. At election time, to be sure, horse race polling predominates, as we think it should. But in between the rush of campaigns, a span which, as we now know, does not have to contract continuously, issues polling is ascendant. One can ask how well each is being done—the task of other chapters in this volume—but one cannot easily question the legitimacy of either issues polling or horse race polling as such. Both now flourish.

Were there too many horse race polls and news stories based on them during the 1988 campaigns? Those who think so probably also think there was too much polling on the Persian Gulf crisis from August 1990 through February 1991. Media polling chases whatever topic is hot at the moment. During the Gulf crisis, national polling organizations asked Americans some 5,000 questions, almost half of them on the crisis itself. During January and February 1991, an extraordinary 75 percent of all survey questions from national polling organizations concerned the crisis. This was excessive. Redundancy in news polling may be a great public service, giving all interested readers a chance to check one set of results against another and get a more complete view. But the events in the Gulf were surely overexplored, just as the presidential horse race of 1988 was examined excessively. Still, there are in journalism worse problems than polling redundancy bred of the competitive instincts of a vigorous, pluralistic press.

News polls are a staple of reporting and public life everywhere in the industrialized world. Michel Brulé, director of the French survey firm BVA, wrote in 1990 that the annual number of opinion surveys conducted for the national press in France rose from 373 to 714 in the 1980s, substantially more than were done in the United States.[8] News polling is also now established in much of the second and third worlds.

These developments are to be welcomed. Some observers may worry about polling on grounds that public life is complex and rich and includes problems that polls cannot capture. Of course, the kind of information that polling, even at its best, can yield is distinctly limited. But what a critical and glorious role it has: trying to find out as well as can be done what people think on matters involving their polity.

Appendix

In 1989 the John F. Kennedy School of Government and the Brookings Institution asked the Roper Center for Public Opinion Research to gather data on news organizations' use of opinion polling and survey research in their news coverage. In particular, what proportion of the organizations are principal sponsors or conducting agencies, or both, for news polls? How much growth has there been since the 1960s in the number of media organizations doing polls and the number of polls conducted? And how does the press employ polls?

To answer these questions, the Roper Center reviewed surveys conducted by other investigators, drew on its data as a public opinion research library, and conducted a new survey among news organizations, asking them how much they poll and how they employ polls.

The first task was to determine which of the news organizations had some substantial involvement in polling for news purposes. We followed a commonsense standard. If, for example, an organization had not conducted more than one poll a year in recent years, we considered it not substantially involved. We are satisfied from conversations with news executives involved in polling that the lack of a precise cut-off for "substantial" did not cause confusion. Once we determined an organization was substantially engaged, the appropriate polling executive was sent a five-page questionnaire inquiring about the organization's operation.

The sample consisted of three groups: major media news organizations, the nation's largest newspapers, and big-city and local television stations.

For major pollsters we selected 13 news organizations acting either alone or in concert (they made up 10 groups): ABC News, CBS News, CNN, NBC News, *New York Times*, *Wall Street Journal*, *Washington Post*, *Los Angeles Times*, *USA Today*, Associated Press, *Time*, *Newsweek*, and *U.S. News and World Report*. At the time the survey was conducted, each organization was active in polling, alone or in concert, except for *U.S. News and World Report*. All ten groups (100 percent response rate) are accounted for in the results.

We excluded the syndicated Gallup and Harris surveys, which are not sponsored by individual newspapers but nonetheless appear in many papers on a regular basis. Gallup and Harris surveys specifically sponsored by single news organizations—surveys conducted for *Newsweek*, for instance—were included.

We also selected the 100 largest-circulation newspapers (excluding 5 that had already been included as major pollsters) as listed in the 1988 *Editor & Publisher International Yearbook*. In practice this meant newspapers with circulations of 115,000 or more. Of the 95 newspapers in the sample, 87 (92 percent) supplied basic information and 47 (49 percent) returned completed questionnaires.

Finally, we selected 54 big-city and local television stations chosen from the 1988 *Broadcasting/Cablecasting Yearbook*. To get a sense of activity independent of that initiated by the networks, we chose every VHF station in Los Angeles, Chicago, and New York, and every fifteenth of the other commercial VHF stations from the list in the *Yearbook*. Fifty-two stations (96 percent) provided basic information, and 16 (30 percent) returned completed questionnaires.

Notes

1. Warren J. Mitofsky, "A Short History of Exit Polls," in Paul J. Lavrakas and Jack K. Holley, eds., *Polling and Presidential Election Coverage* (Newbury Park, Calif.: Sage Publications, 1991), pp. 86–88.

2. Albert H. Cantril, *The Opinion Connection: Polling, Politics, and the Press* (Washington: CQ Press, 1991), pp. 34–35.

3. In 1978 Rippey sent a mail questionnaire to 817 daily newspapers selected randomly from the 1977 *Editor & Publisher Yearbook*. He received responses from 437. See John N. Rippey, "Use of Polls as a Reporting Tool," *Journalism Quarterly*, vol. 57 (Winter 1980), pp. 642–46. In 1986 Demers replicated Rippey's survey; 413 daily newspapers responded to his mail questionnaire. See David Pearce Demers, "Use of Polls in Reporting Changes Slightly since 1978," *Journalism Quarterly*, vol. 64 (Winter 1987), pp. 839–42. In 1989 Holley conducted telephone interviews with a stratified sample of 129 daily newspapers drawn from the 1989 *Editor & Publisher International Yearbook*. Unlike Rippey and Demers, who considered polling a means of gathering information on which to base various kinds of stories, Holley was concerned only with political polling. See Jack K. Holley, "The Press and Political Polling," in Lavrakas and Holley, eds., *Polling and Presidential Election Coverage*, pp. 215–37.

4. Demers, "Use of Polls in Reporting Changes," p. 840.

5. The period for the study was chosen because it included the general election part of a national campaign and the Chicago primary elections of February 28, 1989. Of the 122 stories mentioning polls and surveys, about half were sponsored by the news media. Data are from Henry Brady and are reported in chapter 4.

6. Demers, "Use of Polls in Reporting Changes," p. 841.

7. Tallies by News Surveys Department, *New York Times*.

8. Michel Brulé and Pierre Giacometti, "Opinion Polling in France at the End of the '80s," *Public Perspective* (March–April 1990), p. 19.

Chapter 3

Technology and the Changing Landscape of Media Polls

KATHLEEN A. FRANKOVIC

JUST BEFORE the outbreak of war in the Persian Gulf, at a meeting of CBS News television producers planning news coverage, I was asked whether there would be daily polling of public reaction. The question was serious: the war coverage being considered was, after all, the outgrowth of live network coverage of political conventions and election night. Technically, daily polling was possible, as was measuring opinion several times during a single day. But just as no broadcast news organization conducted such tracking polls during an entire preelection campaign (leaving that to the *Presidential Campaign Hotline Newsletter*), no organization tracked opinion during the entire war, although many conducted multiple polls.

Still, the news media have adapted the methods of election polling to many new uses. Polls have become a major, normal component of reporting. Procedures developed to provide nearly instant surveys after presidential candidate debates have been adapted to measure and report on public reaction to baseball scandals, plane crashes, charges against Supreme Court nominees, summit meetings, and wars.

The long history of many survey questions (including the three famous Gallup items that date from the 1940s—approval of the president's performance, identification with a political party, and naming the country's most important problem) means questionnaires can be assembled quickly by compiling trend questions. Not much investment in developing new questions is needed. The speed in measurement provided by computer-assisted telephone interviewing or by data entry personnel working overnight means that results can be reported minutes after the last interview is completed. For most news media survey organizations, such speed gives a competitive edge.

But many so-called recent innovations in public opinion research have long histories. The first exit poll appears to have been conducted in 1940, when voters in Denver were surveyed in voting booths set up outside precinct polling places. Small-scale panel surveys conducted before and after elections existed before the 1940s, and the first national panel survey was probably conducted during the 1944 presidential election, when the National Opinion Research Corporation conducted pre- and postelection interviews with more than 2,000 adults.[1] Tracking polls, which demand speed in processing and interpretation, resemble the telegraphic samples taken by Gallup in the final days of earlier presidential election campaigns. Even the call-in surveys that use telephone 900 numbers, in their self-selection and availability only to those respondents who learn that a poll is taking place, are not much different from the mail-in questionnaires, usually postcard length, printed in newspapers.

Early observers of the American political scene attributed to newspapers the ability and need to report the public mood. In the nineteenth century James Bryce noted that one of the functions of the American press was to serve as a weathercock of the community's attitudes (the other functions were to be narrator and advocate).[2] As journalists performed these functions, they became innovators in survey research techniques. In 1824 one newspaper printed what was probably the first poll cross-tabulation in a newspaper—the results of a survey of the presidential preferences among passengers on a Mississippi riverboat, cross-tabulated by state of origin, to demonstrate regional differences in preference. In 1923 the *Chicago Tribune* seems to have conducted the first telephone survey when it discovered its street-corner straw poll was missing the wealthier "native" (white protestant) members of the community. In the same campaign the *Tribune* also approximated a panel survey, although the paper actually interviewed different people at the same locations at various times in the campaign.[3]

By the 1970s, telephone surveys had become the methodology of choice as costs declined, more households had telephones, and journalists' interest in survey results increased. As in the earlier days, an important methodological advance came from a news media poll. Warren Mitofsky of CBS News devised a two-stage, random-digit-dial sampling procedure, which was further refined by his former colleague at the Census Bureau,

Joseph Waksberg.[4] The Mitofsky-Waksberg method was first used at the beginning of the CBS News–*New York Times* collaboration in 1975 and has since been adopted by most polling organizations.

New technologies and more pervasive polling have influenced the collecting and reporting of public opinion. For some, the news media's use of these research technologies is a perversion of academic techniques; to others, the shortcuts required by the financial and time constraints in gathering news demand greater creativity on the part of the researcher. An influential academic researcher, Herbert Hyman, wrote about his work with the strategic bombing survey in World War II, summarizing both the constraints and the exhilaration that media researchers today often feel.

> When speed was essential, there were sometimes undesirable consequences. The sample size, the length of the instrument, and the depth of the analysis might have to be curtailed; care might have to be sacrificed. Yet substantial and sophisticated studies were conducted and carefully analyzed despite the tight time schedules. . . . It could be done, and the explanation is basically simple, though it may elude survey researchers reared in a later, more leisurely era. Under pressure and with strong motivation, the wartime staffs learned to be efficient and skillful, thoughtful without becoming obsessive, speedy but not sloppy. It was wonderful training. There were periods of fatigue and frustration when a deadline prevented the pursuit of an interesting analysis, but there were compensations. The deadlines spared us the pains of interminable conceptualizing and analysis, common afflictions in the later era, and there was an exhilarating sense of accomplishment. The need for speed not only improved the skills of the staff but also led to innovations in procedure.[5]

This chapter examines some developments that have changed news coverage of public opinion: exit polls, improvements in computer technology, tracking polls, panel methodologies, and focus groups. The examination has two concerns. First, how do news organizations balance their needs for speed, if not immediacy, in gathering survey results, with the necessity to use recognized survey methodologies? Second, how do they balance rising survey costs and tighter budgets?

The Exit Poll

The exit poll is an invention of the news media. Serious experimentation with this type of survey began in the 1960s at both NBC News and

CBS News, and data files from national general election exit polls date back to 1968. But exit polls did not become a routine part of any network's presidential primary coverage until 1976.[6] Because exit polls allow nearly immediate interpretation of what voting has meant, they are perhaps the most important methodological contribution that news organizations have made to survey research.

Having the results of an exit poll on the same day as the election is not just a matter of being able to call the winner early. The polls also allow editors and producers to plan the kinds of coverage dictated by the outcome. A television producer will know by early afternoon which candidates or consultants to pursue for interviews that night. A newspaper editor will have a sense of how much space to allocate to each reporter. Advance warning of an upset in the making is especially useful.

Exit polls also permit news organizations to put elections into context. Explanations for victory or defeat are no longer the province solely of candidates and their consultants; the voters themselves answer questions about the issues and other factors that motivated their choices. In 1980, for example, many reporters' attributed Ronald Reagan's crushing defeat of President Jimmy Carter to a national "turn to the right." The Reagan campaign entourage also wanted to believe this interpretation. But, as reported on election night and the day after, exit polls across the nation suggested that Americans had not become more conservative. The main reason people said they supported Reagan was that they wanted to reject Carter. The exit data even convinced Reagan's pollster, Richard Wirthlin, who dismissed the theory of a turn to the right a few days after the election.[7]

Methods

Conducting an exit poll is much like conducting any survey—samples need to be selected, interviewers hired and trained, data processed. But the sample size is larger, the time in the field shorter, and the processing and analysis faster. As a result, exit polls have severe constraints. Questionnaires must be brief enough to be completed within a few minutes. They must be especially clear and unambiguous (so they can be administered by paper and pencil, in most cases without interviewer assistance). And although they can theoretically contain open-ended questions, the need for fast processing has forced all major news organizations to rely on closed-end formats.

Good exit polling relies on the principles of probability sampling, with all precincts having a known chance of selection. Precincts are stratified by geographical location, population, and previous voting patterns. In less well designed exit polls, sampling has been done selectively, with precincts chosen by unassisted judgment, or selected to ease the difficulties an interviewer will face. An organization might, for example, choose only precincts that have mirrored the statewide results in previous years. But these, like so-called bellwether counties, have only a 50 percent chance of being accurate again. Or an organization might select a random sample of precincts and eliminate those that would be difficult to poll because of distance, layout, or unfriendly polling officials, replacing them with other precincts. Both of those methods introduce bias, and their results are not projectible to actual election results.

As in any survey, probability selection must extend to the level of the individual. Respondents are usually interviewed at polling places by systematic selection with a random start. Interviewers often work with only sporadic supervision and sometimes with none at all, so training is critical: respondents are anonymous, and exit interviews cannot be verified after the fact by a supervisor, as in-person or telephone interviews can. Because interviewers, as in the early days of household interviewing, choose respondents themselves, they must learn and follow clearly defined procedures. They must remain on duty throughout election day or, if the work is divided between two interviewers, for a major part of it. This can mean standing in a February snowstorm in New Hampshire.

Restrictions

Even an organized, well-designed polling procedure can break down. Often the cause is not that interviewers shirk their responsibilities but that election officials prevent them from carrying out their jobs, charging news organizations with interfering in the election process.

After the 1980 election, critics accused networks of reducing voter turnout on the West Coast because NBC News reported at 8:15 p.m. eastern standard time that Ronald Reagan had won enough electoral votes to win the presidency. Under their authority to regulate elections, several states subsequently passed laws to restrict exit polling, mainly by requiring interviewers to stand so far from the polling place that they would find it impossible to recognize voters or to interview them. These restrictions were challenged in *Daily Herald Co.* v. *Munro*, which involved a Washington state law. The state claimed that the restrictions were warranted because reporting exit poll results violated the sanctity of the election process. But a federal court ruled that because the state could show no evidence that the process of conducting an exit poll interfered with people's ability to vote, the law violated First Amendment press rights.[8] Other states have passed similar legislation, but all such restrictions have been challenged in court or are not enforced because mechanisms are lacking, court orders have prevented enforcement, or administrations have changed. Restrictions are, however, sometimes imposed by individual jurisdictions and election officials. No matter how they are imposed or by whom, they can result in unreliable data.

Exit poll interviewers also face occasional bad weather and difficulties in reaching voters because of multiple exits and multiple precincts in one polling location. All affect the ability to sample voters accurately. Research by CBS News indicates that bad weather and interviewers located a long distance from the voting place harm the accuracy of exit poll results in sample precincts.

Do Voters Lie?

In addition to the difficulties of sampling and collecting data, what else affects the accuracy of exit polls? Are voters telling (or writing) the truth about their voting? Are they willing to answer questions at all?

From 30 to 50 percent of all voters who should be interviewed in a given exit poll either refuse to participate or are missed by interviewers. Failure to respond is higher in the largest cities and lower in rural states outside the Northeast. Nonresponse differs little by sex or race but does differ by age: the oldest voters, for whatever reasons, have been the least likely to respond. The greater chances that an older voter will fail to respond may result from skepticism or lack of confidence in the interviewing process, fear, or even the inability to read the questionnaire because of illiteracy or poor eyesight. Necessarily, then, if voting preference is to some extent dependent on the voter's age, an exit poll will estimate election results inaccurately unless adjustments are made to compensate for age-related failure to respond.

Most people who refuse to be interviewed do so for personal rather than ideological or principled reasons. Interviewers have noted some unwillingness to participate because results of exit polls have been used to project winners before polls in western states have closed, but relatively few people refuse to be interviewed for that reason. Nor do they seem to fear a breach of privacy. Even though questionnaires are often administered with paper and pencil (to allow many respondents to participate at the same time and make interviewing possible during periods of heavy voting), the document preserves the secrecy of the ballot box. Respondents do not have to publicly state their preferences, the reason for those preferences, or their demographic characteristics.

Face-to-face interviews, however, can be another matter. In the 1989 gubernatorial election in Virginia, when Douglas Wilder, a black Democrat, defeated James Coleman, a white Republican, one exit poll that questioned respondents face to face underestimated the share of the vote received by Coleman. The pollster concluded that many respondents said they voted for the black Democrat when in fact they voted for the white Republican. Another exit poll that used pencil and paper also underestimated Coleman's percentage, but the estimate was closer to the actual result. Researchers decided that the verbal, face-to-face interview in the first poll created much of its accuracy problem.[9]

But if in fact exit polls have difficulty gauging the outcome of black-white elections with their usual accuracy, part of the explanation may be the complications of a racially tinged election. For a poll to be accurate in these circumstances, it must reflect both turnout and preference. That means pollsters must estimate the number of votes that will be cast in sample precincts as well as the outcome in those precincts. In Chicago and New York, whites and blacks vote at different times of the day, producing different estimates of overall turnout at different times of the day. As for results, there may be more spoiled ballots in black areas. CBS News analyses indicate that voter response rates also differ because of the race of the interviewer: same-race interviewers get better cooperation. Because the exit poll relies on voter cooperation for its accuracy, theoretically the higher the response rate, the more accurate the estimate.

Although lying by respondents is always a possibility, it does not seem to occur on any massive scale. In 1980 Mike Royko, then a columnist with the *Chicago Sun-Times*, suggested a few days before the Illinois primary that exit polls were taking the fun out of politics and that if pollsters showed up at readers' precincts, people should lie about everything—who they were as well as who they voted for.[10] Royko was taken seriously by the news organizations that conduct exit polls, if not by the public. CBS News and the *New York Times* conducted a quick telephone survey in the Chicago area to find out if people were aware of Royko's suggestion and, if they were, how they reacted to it. Most who were aware of the column simply dismissed it as a joke. At the polls, exit poll interviewers indicated no obvious evidence of lying. It is more difficult to lie when responding to an exit poll than it is to refuse to participate. Refusals pose a greater threat to accuracy than deliberate misrepresentation.

Racially divided elections (or other instances that could cause people to be less willing to report socially unacceptable voting) could be becoming less a threat to accuracy in polling. Despite pollsters' and journalists' fears, there was no evidence of any unwillingness to report voting for former Ku Klux Klan Grand Wizard David Duke in the 1991 Louisiana gubernatorial runoff, the most recent racially tinged election. The vote distribution in the exit poll precisely matched the final tally.

Overall, inaccuracy in exit polls is more the result of sloppy design or unclear questions than of false responses. If questionnaires are too long, people may refuse to participate or may stop answering questions toward the end of the survey. On two-sided questionnaires, 3 percent of all respondents fail to turn the page over.

The Exit Poll's Future

Television networks have agreed not to broadcast vote-related results from exit polls before most polls close in each state. And since 1990, with the pooling of exit poll and other election night data collection by ABC, CBS, CNN, and NBC, calling races before a competitor does is no longer possible. The networks created Voter Research & Surveys to divide the costs of statewide exit polls and other data gathering for election night estimations. VRS has saved the financially strapped broadcast networks millions of dollars each. And CNN, which had never invested in this polling technology, has been able to participate as an equal without investing heavily in new equipment, personnel, and procedures.

The formation of VRS has forced the creation of a single set of procedures. CBS, ABC, and NBC had developed different methods of data collection, methods that extended to the substance and design of questionnaires. But with VRS as the sole source of information, the networks had to standardize presentation and questions. (A network can choose to purchase additional questions. In 1990, only CBS News, in conjunction with the *New York Times*, bought additional questions. In the 1992 primaries, all four networks purchased unilateral questions.)

Some of the most intense discussions about the content of the VRS exit poll questionnaires have focused on the wording of demographic questions. ABC, CBS, and NBC had each developed its own categories for age, religion, and income. None precisely matched another, and each version could be supported on theoretical as well as traditional grounds. ABC News, for example, grouped age by decades (younger than 20, 20–29, 30–39, and so forth). CBS News used four groupings (18–29, 30–44, 45–59, 60 or older). NBC News had an additional category for those age 65 and older. Again, NBC traditionally asked in what religion a respondent was reared. ABC and CBS asked for current religious affiliation. Income categories differed. The importance of ethnic identification varied. In the short term, resolving these differences satisfied no one network, except perhaps CNN, which had no previous trends to save.

Although VRS is now the sole source of exit poll information for network news broadcasts, the formation of the pool has made information more widely available than formerly because the networks encourage subscriptions to the service from local print and broadcast organizations. But ironically, the uniformity of the information and its availability for less money may have diminished its value. Instead of spending significant parts of evenings reporting the primaries in 1992, the networks provided only brief updates and late-night half hours. This trend toward briefer coverage began in 1986, when only CBS presented a full night of election coverage. In 1988 the CBS News all-night coverage of the Super Tuesday primaries may have had as much to do with economics as altruism—the network's Tuesday night entertainment lineup was rated lower than those of ABC and NBC and it stood to lose less advertising revenue from cancelling the shows. In 1992, CBS reduced its prime time coverage of Super Tuesday results to an hour.

More cuts in network election coverage are foreseeable. The Iowa caucuses and the New Hampshire primary have not received the saturation coverage they have had in the past. There has been more pool coverage of the conventions, which have diminished in importance. Cutbacks in basic coverage, however, are meant to coincide with increases in campaign and election analysis, and exit polls, even if limited in number, still provide those analytic data.

Computers and Telephone Interviewing

Currently, interviewers for exit polls read respondents' answers over the telephone to operators who enter the responses into a data file. This process occurs at least three times during an election day and could benefit from new technology. Although use of bar code readers by interviewers in the field, touch-tone data entry by respondents, and data entry on laptop computers by interviewers themselves have not yet been used during exit polls, each innovation has been discussed.

Just as the exit poll developed in response to the broadcast media's need to have reportable election results as quickly as possible, other innovations in survey research have also been adopted and adapted. Newer, faster computers have changed the way surveys are conducted; and the availability of powerful personal computers has made that technology available to more news organizations to conduct more polls in smaller markets at less cost. But technological advances also bring potential drawbacks. Too much information that will never find its way into print or onto the air is now gathered. And news organizations may be tempted to accept less than accurate information simply because it has become easier to collect.

Computer-Assisted Interviewing and Data Collection

When CBS News established its in-house survey unit in the late 1960s, it depended on an IBM mainframe computer to generate samples and process data. Operators punched responses from paper questionnaires onto computer cards, and computer programmers wrote proprietary analysis packages. By 1975 when the CBS News/*New York Times* polls began, procedures had not changed very much. Since then, however, inexpensive analysis packages have become available to users of personal computers. The punch card has been superseded by direct data entry and then by direct input of respondents' answers by the interviewers themselves. Such computer-assisted telephone interviewing (CATI) was first used by market research and other organizations that conduct daily surveys. News organizations that conducted polls themselves and only in response to news events at first found the hardware for the system too costly. In addition, while CATI does reduce the time between interview and analysis, it requires more programming before interviewing begins. So questionnaires for the overnight surveys that many organizations conduct are often written so close to the start of interviewing that a CATI system cannot be used.

The implications of CATI and other developments in personal computing for news surveys are twofold. First, processing time has been reduced and specialization in processing has disappeared. Programs that had to be custom written can now be purchased inexpensively. This has allowed smaller staffs. Second, faster survey processing has meant more timely reporting of results. ABC News reported public opinion on 1984's first presidential debate less than an hour after it ended. Since then, instant analysis has indeed become almost instant. Morning papers can report not only the content of a debate but also the first public reactions to it, a capability *USA Today* exploited to print reaction poll results the morning after the U.S. bombing of Libya and the morning after the beginning of the Persian Gulf airwar.

Overnight surveys emphasize speed over depth. They must. Many contain just fifteen important questions and often far fewer. Respondents are generally those adults who are home at the time the call is placed. Callbacks, if made at all, are limited. This means the sample may not be representative, although this shortcoming is often at least partly corrected through weighting. Questions are usually written quickly, although many of the most common are trend questions that do not change.

More frequent, even hourly, surveys are possible. During the war in the Persian Gulf, CBS News and the *New York Times*, as well as other news organizations, sampled public opinion immediately before and after the first Scud missile attack on Israel on January 17, 1991. Similarly, a poll can examine the impact of a presidential address by coding the time an interview is conducted.

There are prospects for even faster processing. About 80 percent of U.S. households have touch-tone telephones. Responses to taped or live questions could be entered directly by the respondent. Taped questions, although they raise questions of whether an appropriate respondent has been reached and preclude any rapport between interviewer and respondent, could slash polling costs. Giving respondents hand-held transmitters or devices wired to central units could record answers to questions and continuing reactions to commercials and events. Those results would be processed immediately. Although those using the devices would not constitute a national sample, their reactions could form the core of a television or newspaper analysis.

This newfound speed in reporting survey results has altered the understanding of public opinion on the part of reporters and the public. Public opinion is now considered more changeable, and change is expected (this is the justification for conducting tracking polls, discussed later.) Polls also become part of the analysis much sooner, so expert opinion about the impact of a debate or other political event becomes less relevant. That change may be good or bad for the political system, but it does mean that politics will be viewed differently.

Even the knowledge that poll results will be available the next morning, or perhaps the next hour, can change reporting. After the first 1984 debate between President Ronald Reagan and Democratic challenger Walter Mondale, CBS News correspondents refused to comment on how each had fared, unwilling perhaps to be second-guessed by poll results. Not until the next day, when it became clear that voters had thought the underdog Mondale had won, did CBS News report the debate as a Mondale success and a Reagan problem.

Another consequence of the rapid availability of survey data is, paradoxically, that reporters have become more familiar with what to expect from public opinion even as it becomes more changeable. Before the Persian Gulf War, reporters studied public opinion in previous conflicts, especially during the Vietnam War. They consequently expected the public immediately to rally round the president and support the attack, whatever the doubts that had been expressed before it began.[11] And that is, in fact, what happened. The second stage of public opinion predicted by the press corps—that support would begin to vanish as American deaths increased—of course, never took place.

Journalists' familiarity with public opinion research has also reduced expectations about how much the public actually knows. Most journalists expect Americans to know little about events overseas, the details of public policies, the presidential candidates, or even basic geography. These diminished expectations may mean that they tell Americans less than they did in the days before rapid and frequent polling.

Improvements in Data Processing and Larger Polls

Technological advances have not only allowed faster processing of data, but faster processing of enormous amounts of data. More than 100,000 exit poll interviews have been conducted and processed in a single day. In 1988 the ABC News/*Washington Post* poll interviewed more than 12,000 registered voters in fifty states and the District of Columbia in two and one-half weeks and released the results the evening before the second George Bush–Michael Dukakis debate.[12] The major purpose of the poll was to help estimate the likely outcome of the election in each jurisdiction, so sample size was based on the heterogeneity of the jurisdiction and the expected closeness of the election. There were more than 500 respondents in some states, and only 45 in the District of Columbia. Of course there was never any doubt that the District of Columbia would vote for the Democratic ticket.

The main criticisms of the fifty-state poll were not about its methodology although interviews spread over two and one-half weeks were too long to fix the status of a changing campaign and the sampling error for states with small samples was too great to gauge the outcome in the state one way or another. The main criticism was instead political, that the timing of the poll's release may have cost Dukakis the election.

The night before the Dukakis-Bush debate the results of the poll led ABC's evening news, and discussion of the results and the current status of the campaign took up much of the broadcast. The news that Dukakis was losing badly in electoral votes just a week before the election weakened his performance in the debate, according to his staff. And the results of the poll formed the backdrop for the questioners and the debate audience. The next day the debate itself shared the news spotlight with the poll. The existence of the poll raised questions about the effects of polling for the campaign and the possible impact on the election itself.[13] But the poll was only one source for the fifty-state classification that ABC News and the *Washington Post* produced: other sources included aggregate past results, local polls, and conversations with political experts. And the same fifty-state poll conducted in 1984 had produced no such outrage. The difference in 1988 was that people believed the report had crippled the Dukakis campaign. In 1984 the outcome and the magnitude of the Reagan reelection victory had not been in doubt; in 1988 there was at least some question about the outcome.

Reaction Surveys and Crises

Too often speed in polling is considered a liability, an inevitable cause of inaccuracy. But the rapid measurement of public opinion has some benefits, especially for understanding public reaction to crisis. What may have been the first reaction poll was conducted by Hadley Cantril in 1938, during a period of grave concern about events in Europe and possible war. Cantril measured reaction to Orson Welles's Halloween radio broadcast, "War of the Worlds," which vividly dramatized an invasion of the United States by Martians and had set off panic among some Americans. Cantril distinguished those listeners who panicked from those who did not, discovering differences in their backgrounds and the ways they attempted to validate the information about a Martian takeover, providing information about human response to crises.[14]

Herbert Hyman justified speed in his research during World War II on still other grounds: "Our prime concern was practical, not scholarly, and we believed from past experience that we could be quick without being hasty, thoughtful without becoming obsessive, thorough without engaging in interminable analysis. It never would have occurred to us back then that a survey researcher needed six months or a year to design a survey and another year or two to analyze the findings."[15]

Hyman's words could as easily have been spoken by any media researcher who operates under severe deadlines in unusual locations and who must sometimes ignore the latest methodologies and technologies. A few days after the U.S. invasion of Grenada in 1983, Warren Mitofsky of CBS News drew a grid across the island, selected an area sample, and flew to St. George (the island's capital). He typed the questionnaire on his way and hired interviewers through his cabdriver and a medical school librarian. Screening took place in a training session in which prospective interviewers were asked to read aloud. The day after he arrived the interviewers went out with quotas to fill and strict rules about household selection. The results were hand tallied and reported the next day. Grenadans expressed support for the U.S. invasion, something that was in doubt in the days following that action.

CBS News sent Nancy Belden to Panama soon after the U.S. invasion in 1990.[16] Within a week after the invasion, experienced Panamanian interviewers were in the field. Belden improvised a mix of sampling designs to achieve access to households. Typically, in Latin America and other areas less dependent on telephones, face-to-face interviews are the only accurate way of sampling. But after the invasion, wealthier neighborhoods were patrolled and off limits to unescorted interviewers, so telephone sampling was adopted for them. Later in 1990, at the World Association for Public Opinion Research Seminar in Caracas, Venezuela, it was proposed that the procedure be adopted generally in Latin America.

Sometimes the latest technologies are inappropriate. At times of breaking news, and in nonindustrial societies, news researchers must borrow techniques from earlier generations—in the spirit of Herbert Hyman.

The Tracking Poll

The most common "reaction" poll does rely on the increased capacity for polling and the increasing speed of analysis. The tracking poll provides the possibility of daily measurements of public opinion. Journalistic use of the tracking poll is the result of two factors: a perceived need to know public preferences before an election and an assumption that people are unstable in their political preferences, react to events, and will change their preferences in response. Tracking polls are also a way to merge relatively sophisticated polling technology with the needs of a news organization for daily reports.

News organizations' concerns about the speed of changes in public sentiment stem in part from memories of the 1980 presidential election. The weekend before the election, polls suggested that President Jimmy Carter and challenger Ronald Reagan were neck and neck. The ten-point Reagan victory margin on election day shocked many journalists. News organizations that stopped polling the week before (or even the Saturday before) were stunned by the magnitude of the movement. But tracking polls conducted through the evening before election day had documented the change.

Tracking involves polling a new sample each day. For political campaigns that may mean as few as 150 voters interviewed daily, with results aggregated over the preceding three days to achieve what is thought to be the best measurement of a candidate's current standing. This rolling sample, in theory, will pick up any movement in public support while controlling for the small daily sample size. Each day a new sample's results are added in, and results from the least current day are dropped.

The main reason for aggregation into three-day units is that pollsters lack confidence in the small samples. And the problem becomes more difficult if subgroups—working women or urban blacks, for example— are the focus of analysis. Media organizations cannot risk much inaccuracy and usually conduct tracking polls with much larger samples. In a tracking poll conducted the week before the 1988 presidential election, CBS News routinely interviewed nearly 1,000 people a day, aggregated results over only a two-day period, and occasionally reported results from one day's sample only. A sample size of 1,000 yields many subgroups that are large enough for reasonable analysis.

In the past few years many campaign pollsters have also increased sample sizes to get more reliable estimates and larger subgroups, although because of the expense, campaigns rarely interview more than 300 people a day. Such a sample is more than adequate for a small, relatively homogeneous area, but causes problems in assessing opinion in larger, urban heterogeneous areas. Candidates' pollsters have made other adjustments. For example, many do not interview on Friday nights, believing that the distribution of voters reached is older and more conservative than at other times. Conducting a tracking poll, however, means more than interviewing enough people or deciding when to interview. If it is restricted to randomly selected telephone numbers, new every day, the only people sampled will be those who are relatively easy to reach. There are often differences in political preferences and positions on issues between those who are often home and those who are not.[17] Consequently, a good tracking poll includes interviews with people reached from a new independent random sample of telephone numbers, as well as with appointments made previously and interviews with people whose telephones earlier went unanswered or were busy. Each day's interviews are weighted separately to national population parameters and then combined.

Television news organizations began using tracking polls in the 1984 presidential campaign. ABC News/*Washington Post* tracked voters' preferences in New Hampshire in the week before the state's primaries and reported the increase in support for Gary Hart following his surprising second-place finish to Walter Mondale in the Iowa caucuses. The movement toward Hart in New Hampshire, where voters were paying close attention to the election, long predated any shift in national polls of Democrats. Only ABC conducted tracking polls before the 1984 primaries, although CBS conducted one before the general election. By 1988 CBS and the Gallup Poll joined ABC in tracking opinion in key primaries. For the most part, television news tracking polls have been accurate in indicating change and predicting winners.

There are some criticisms of tracking polls, however. Polls conducted before primaries, with their brief questionnaires, generally provide little beyond rankings, making them useful for television stories but less so for newspaper analyses. In addition, television can report partial results on an 11:30 p.m. broadcast or final results the morning of election day, neither of which is amenable to the deadlines of most morning newspapers (although *USA Today* has successfully reported polls conducted the night before). Finally, some national newspapers have expressed dismay at the prospect of sponsoring daily measurements of preference. Some have even editorialized against them.

The use of tracking polls in news programs does promote uniformity of poll reporting, at least within a single news organization. Poll results are presented in a similar manner each day, with each report taking approximately the same amount of time and incorporating the same graphic background. Except when significant changes occur in preferences (and given the combination of several days' samples, any change is likely to appear smaller than it really is), the tracking poll report can take on a sameness that either makes the results more believable or just more boring.

Panel Surveys

Panel surveys consist of interviews with the same people at two or more times. In 1938 George Gallup used a panel survey to measure changing opinion in the New York gubernatorial election. In 1939 the Psychological Corporation, a pioneer in attitude research for business and marketing applications, conducted a panel survey on a New Jersey referendum.[18] These surveys were conducted to test methodology and determine whether people were telling the truth. Later academic panel surveys focused on the impact of campaign messages on voters' choices. Panel surveys by news organizations are conducted to improve reporters' ability to understand change. Change is news and is part of what reporters care about. Panel surveys are most effective in helping reporters understand reactions to a specific event—a campaign, an election, a crisis— and that is how most news organizations use them. Panels compensate for some of the deficiencies of overnight polls.

Since 1976 CBS News and the *New York Times* have conducted panel surveys before and after presidential elections. In 1976 the fascination with panels was so great that they were built into the methodology for interviewing, with as many as one-half of the households called each month contacted again the following month. That methodology proved unworkable, but reinterviews have been employed in many nonelection contexts, including before and after the start of the Persian Gulf war (to discover the extent of change in support for the war) and before and after the hearings conducted to explore charges of sexual harassment against Clarence Thomas. Panels are also efficient sources for interviewing representative samples of the public on short notice: respondents have already been selected and can be followed, and demographic information has already been collected. But the most common news media use of panel surveys has been during political campaigns.

The Gallup Organization and other polling firms used panels in their search for reasons the polls went wrong in 1948, when they predicted an easy victory for New York Governor Thomas Dewey over President Harry Truman. And as mentioned earlier, the *Chicago Tribune*, which began conducting polls early in the century, attempted something like a panel survey while covering the 1923 mayoral election in Chicago. The *Tribune* sent reporters back to the same neighborhoods it had polled before in an effort to record the amount of change in preference that had taken place during the campaign.

The 1980 election demonstrates the specific news value of panel surveys. After the 1960 election and the first televised presidential debates, pollsters sensed that, barring a major gaffe by a candidate, voters will say the candidate they support has done the best job during a debate. But it was unclear whether the connection could be demonstrated or whether preference could be altered by the debate itself. In the 1980 election CBS News conducted a panel survey of registered voters the weekend before the October Carter-Reagan debate. More than 80 percent of the same people were then reinterviewed immediately following the debate. That panel design permitted one simple but very important cross-tabulation: perception of the debate by actual predebate preference rather than memories of predebate preference reported afterward. The hypothesis that people filtered reactions to a debate through their predebate feelings could be confirmed. Additionally, it was possible to compare preferences before and after the debate so that specific change in candidate support could be measured.

This design is now typical in evaluations after a debate. And the finding that voters view debates through a haze of favoritism for one candidate or another is also generally known to journalists. When interviews conducted after 1984's first debate between Ronald Reagan and Walter Mondale indicated that barely half the predebate Reagan supporters believed he had won, it was viewed as a serious setback for the president. Two days later, after those polls and other reports legitimized concern among Reagan supporters, another CBS News/*New York Times* panel found that only one-quarter of predebate Reagan supporters now believed their candidate had won. Half thought Mondale had.

Another important use for a panel survey design occurred in 1980. Political observers had been surprised by the Reagan landslide. Panels were used to find those voters whose preferences had changed or who had decided in the last week of the campaign not to vote. Journalists needed to answer three questions: Who changed and why, and could the polls be trusted at all? The polls of 1980 were being examined with the same skepticism as those of 1948 had been.

The postelection panel indicated that one of every five registered voters changed his or her mind between the first interview and the election, either not voting or changing preference. These voters had been predisposed to vote for Carter, but among those who finally voted there was a shift to Reagan. Voters justified the change by referring to their rethinking of political events and their perceptions of the economy and the situation of the U.S. hostages in Iran. The preelection polls had been accurate in measuring opinion, but they had not been concluded closely enough to the election.

Focus Groups

In a focus group, people are brought together to examine issues, products, and (particularly for political campaigns) advertising themes. The discussions that occur in these groups (usually twelve to fifteen carefully selected people) and the changes in opinion that occur during the discussions provide information to advertisers, marketers, and campaigns on how to shape their themes and arguments.

Focus groups are sometimes used to pretest a poll questionnaire, especially when the subject matter is atypical. In these instances, group participants are led by a facilitator through certain topics, and the ensuing discussion may yield themes and dimensions that are then addressed by closed-end poll questions.

For news media, focus groups give context for the percentages produced by multiple-choice questions in telephone polls. They also provide answers to questions such as "Why do you think that?" During the 1984 campaigns the *Wall Street Journal* relied almost exclusively on the focus group for access to the minds of voters. Throughout the spring and fall the paper interviewed voters and quoted from group discussions. Al Hunt, the *Journal's* Washington bureau chief, defended the practice and argued that the focus group was superior to competitors' public opinion polls.[19] By 1988 the *Journal* had joined NBC News for opinion polls, but the practice of merging the comments of focus group participants with public opinion poll results confirmed the newspaper's earlier preference for focus groups.

No other news organization has relied as heavily on the focus group and no other routinely hires political polling firms to interview the public. When other organizations seek voters' discussion of issues in conjunction with political polling results, they adapt the focus group to a more news-oriented use.

Often news organizations conduct quasi focus groups, interviewing people who have already been respondents in a survey. This device is used frequently by the *New York Times* and *USA Today* and less often by television networks. It is standard news polling practice to ask respondents who have been randomly selected as part of a national sample if they would allow a reporter to call at a later date for more opinions. In the case of the *Times*, selected comments from follow-up interviews are incorporated into the poll story, either to answer "Why do you think that?" or to use a person to represent a particular group—a black conservative, for example, or a Republican who is pro-choice on abortion.

Television news uses quasi focus groups much less often because the cost of adding individual context to a broadcast poll story far exceeds that of the dozen or so additional telephone calls a print reporter makes. At the end of an interview, interviewers usually ask respondents only whether a reporter might call them again, not whether they are willing to appear on camera (relatively few are willing when the follow-up call is made). If a respondent agrees to a television interview, a reporter, producer, and crew must be sent. If the respondent is not near a major city, the cost of transporting the crew can be excessive, so the technique is used only on rare occasions, principally when the respondent represents a trend discovered in the poll. Interviewing someone recently unemployed, for example, in a story about the impact of a recession puts a face to the poll numbers.

Some local television stations, such as WCBS in New York City, have brought up to a dozen respondents into a studio for an hour-long taped discussion, with the material edited to supplement several evenings of poll reporting. But it has been necessary to call as many as 200 potential panel participants (who have already agreed that a reporter could call them again) to find a dozen who are willing to come to the studio to be taped.

Because of such costs, television producers have resorted to other reporting strategies without a direct connection to the sample. The most common is to send crews from various bureaus to ask passersby how they feel about the president's performance or to name the problem facing the country that bothers them most. In 1991 a new television program on the Lifetime cable channel, "The Great American TV Poll," used this technique extensively in conjunction with a regularly scheduled national poll to find out Americans' feelings about everything from the Kennedy family and the attractiveness of big muscles on women to more traditional subjects such as abortion and national health insurance. Television news organizations have also formed their own quasi focus groups, recruiting participants from shopping malls, matching them to some formula for representativeness, and interviewing them.

Some survey researchers have objected to linking individual comments and survey results because the stories may imply that poll respondents risk being quoted even when they do not specifically give permission for the callback interview. Other critics suggest that the practice confuses the audience about what came from the survey and what from the post-survey interview. But television producers and newspaper editors reply that the presentation of poll results without adding "real people" makes a boring report.

Conclusion

News media polls can move in either of two directions, cutting back on survey research because of financial constraints or using newer technologies and innovations in opinion measurement. But decisions will depend on news needs and a willingness to take account of the standards of survey research, even when they may be costly or restrict potential entertainment value.

News polls have so far taken advantage of new technologies and have developed some of their own. In the future, shrinking news budgets may mean that the proportion of new polling developments adapted from outside news organizations may very well increase.

In one way, new technology threatens to overwhelm, or at least pollute, the survey process. Devices can now record opinion via telephone, for instance, through calls made to one of several 900 telephone numbers, each of which represents a different point of view. The technique first came to the attention of politicians when ABC News solicited opinions on who won the 1980 Carter-Reagan debate. Since then these numbers have been used to record opinions on the value of the United Nations (ABC News), whether to replace the national anthem ("CBS This Morning"), whether to kill Larry the Lobster ("Saturday Night Live"), and whether there is too much sex in music videos (MTV). CNN "PrimeNews" has regularly asked a news-related call-in question. In January 1992 CBS News conducted an 800-number call-in following the president's State of the Union message. The broadcast following the address combined the call-in with a more scientific reaction poll, interviews with callers, and prepackaged stories about the state of the country.

The 800 and 900 numbers are convenient tools for involving the viewing public with the television program and engaging people who are otherwise isolated and passive watchers (and the 900 numbers may even generate income for a news organization). The surveys simulate opinion polls, and since they bring in large numbers of calls, they give the impression of validity. But unless the results are properly labeled as the opinions only of those who have called, they can be misinterpreted as representing the entire country.

One other technique that is among the newly devised telephone-related technologies is the registering of responses to prerecorded questions by pressing digits on a touch-tone phone. Efficiencies in conducting ordinary public opinion polls could be achieved by selecting respondents and then giving them prerecorded questions. Also about to be marketed are new devices directly attached to televisions. They allow viewers to place orders for advertised products, participate in game shows, and get more information from advertisers. They could just as easily register opinions about what is being broadcast.

Although the subjects of news polling will increasingly range beyond elections, polls will continue to use the election model. At least in the short term, the first choices for measuring public opinion will continue to be the overnight poll and the panel survey. But in the next decade, innovations are likely to be forced by news organizations' need to control costs, especially at the broadcast networks. They may use smaller samples and take short cuts. There will be the temptation to substitute self-selected call-ins for true measurements of public opinion.

Measuring public opinion will still be important, although justifications by news managers may have more to do with a desire to involve the audience than a need to know and report information. But by appealing to that audience through presenting poll results, news organizations will continue to link Americans together and demonstrate the relative coherence or incoherence of American opinion.

Notes

1. Herbert H. Hyman, *Taking Society's Measure: A Personal History of Survey Research* (Russell Sage, 1991), p. 143.

2. James Bryce, *The American Commonwealth*, vol. 2 (Macmillan, 1910), p. 275.

3. *Chicago Tribune*, March 8–April 1, 1923.

4. The Mitofsky-Waksberg approach involves a two-stage selection design. The first stage takes a pure random sample of telephone exchanges in the United States, stratified

by region and population density, with four random digits appended to the exchange. This sample is then screened for households with telephones. If calls to a number reach a household, that number is retained in the sample. In subsequent surveys, by changing the final two digits of each screened telephone number (usually by adding a nonrecurring integer to each successively generated telephone number), pollsters can reach a set number of households from each cluster in each survey. See Joseph Waksberg, "Sampling Methods for Random Digit Dialing," *Journal of the American Statistical Association*, vol. 73 (March 1976), pp. 40–46.

5. Hyman, *Taking Society's Measure*, p. 53.

6. Mark R. Levy, "The Methodology and Performance of Election Day Polls," *Public Opinion Quarterly*, vol. 47 (Spring 1983), pp. 54–67.

7. "Reagan's Pollster Says Carter's Leadership Was Key Issue," *New York Times*, November 6, 1980, p. 26.

8. *Daily Herald Co.* v. *Munro*, 838 F.2d 380 (1988). The Everett *Herald*, a Washington state paper, was the named plaintiff in the case, but the parties bringing the suit included the three broadcast networks, the *New York Times*, and the *Washington Post*, which owns the *Herald*.

9. Michael Traugott and Vincent Price, "Exit Polls in the 1989 Virginia Gubernatorial Race: Where Did They Go Wrong?" *Public Opinion Quarterly*, vol. 56 (Summer 1992), pp. 245–53.

10. Mike Royko, *Chicago Sun-Times*, March 1980.

11. The phrase "rally round" was common in John E. Mueller's *War, Presidents, and Public Opinion* (University Press of America, 1985), which had become required reading before the war began.

12. "ABC News World News Tonight," October 12, 1988; and Paul Taylor and Richard Morin, "Poll Indicates Bush Has Big Electoral Vote Lead," *Washington Post*, October 13, 1988, pp. A1, A22.

13. The criticisms continued long after the election and included a discussion at a conference sponsored by Harvard University the following year.

14. Hadley Cantril, *The Invasion from Mars: A Study in the Psychology of Panic* (Princeton University Press, 1940).

15. Hyman, *Taking Society's Measure*, p. 109.

16. Belden's father, Joe Belden, was an innovator when he began the Texas poll for a consortium of newspapers in the 1940s. He later developed polling in Mexico.

17. Robert M. Groves and Robert L. Kahn, *Surveys by Telephone: A National Comparison with Personal Interviews* (Academic Press, 1979); and Warren J. Mitofsky, "The 1980 Pre-Election Polls: A Review of Disparate Methods and Results," paper prepared for the 1981 annual conference of the American Statistical Association.

18. Hyman, *Taking Society's Measure*, p. 197.

19. Remarks made at the 1982 annual meeting of the American Political Science Association.

Chapter 4

Polling Pitfalls: Sources of Error in Public Opinion Surveys

HENRY E. BRADY AND GARY R. ORREN

P UBLIC OPINION about public opinion polls—especially their accuracy—is sharply divided. Cynics regard polls as hopelessly
flawed. Their skepticism is frequently accompanied by the comment that
"nobody ever polled me." Trusting souls accept polls with unquestioning
faith. And, of course, observers condemn polls one moment and cite them
uncritically the next, depending on how a poll accords with their point
of view. Such pieties and absolutes must make way for more sober assessment. Polls are not as unreliable as the harshest critics assert, but
the sources of error are many.[1]

To begin with, polls aim to measure intangible, subjective phenom-
ena—attitudes, feelings, beliefs, emotions—and, as V. O. Key, Jr., wrote,
"To speak with precision of public opinion is a task not unlike coming to
grips with the Holy Ghost."[2] The mass surveys used to measure these
elusive opinions are imperfect instruments, bound to introduce error into
the exercise. When these polls are conducted by news organizations,
special difficulties arise. The mating of the worlds of survey research and
journalism has created a troubled union.

Our thanks to Martin Petri, Mary Jane Rose, and Brian Silver for their help in preparing
this chapter, and to Glen Dempsey and Owen Shapiro for permitting us to draw upon their
unpublished work. We especially appreciate the efforts of Robert Eisinger throughout this
project.

Survey Research Meets Journalism

There is an inherent mismatch between the ethos of survey research and the ethos of journalism. A good way to understand the difference is to compare scholars' and reporters' attitudes toward errors. Statisticians recognize two types of errors. A Type II error is mistakenly to reject a true hypothesis that changes our beliefs about the world. For example, suppose that George Bush's popularity—as a hypothetical census of all Americans would measure it—has fallen by 10 percentage points. But suppose too that in a poll of a sample of Americans his popularity has dropped by only 4 points, with a margin of error of plus or minus 6 points. A survey analyst would be strongly inclined to say that no significant drop has occurred: the poll indicated a drop of only 4 points and the margin of error of 6 points may mean the true drop is zero. The analyst therefore would mistakenly reject a true hypothesis. A Type I error is to mistakenly accept a false hypothesis—to assert, for instance, that Bush's popularity had fallen significantly based on a poll when in fact a census of the American public would show that his popularity had not declined at all.

Academic survey researchers, a cautious bunch, would rather commit a Type II error than a Type I. That is, in our example they would rather make the mistake of arguing for no drop in George Bush's popularity when a census would indicate that there had been in fact a drop rather than arguing for a drop when a census would indicate that there had not been one. They prefer to miss a discovery than accept an untrue hypothesis. Accordingly, they subject a hypothesis to detailed and stringent tests of statistical significance before accepting it. The American criminal justice system works in much the same way: "innocent until proven guilty" means the court would rather let a guilty person go free (a Type II error) than convict an innocent one (a Type I error). This methodological caution makes statistics and jury trials slow, risk-averse methods of analysis.

Journalists operate within a rather different ethos. They would rather commit a Type I error than a Type II. They get paid to deliver news on a daily deadline and hate to let an interesting story slip through their fingers. Because someone might scoop them, they cannot afford to caress the data at hand or wait for more. As former *Washington Post* reporter Carl Bernstein has said, "The greatest felony in the news business today . . . is to be behind, or to miss, a major story; or more precisely, to seem behind, or to seem in danger of missing, a major story. So speed and quantity substitute for thoroughness and quality, for accuracy and context."[3] Consequently, reporters often extrapolate events into trends—a hot summer becomes evidence for global warming, a handful of cancer cases demonstrates the ill effects of pesticides, a welfare queen reveals the defects in public assistance programs, a good showing in the Iowa caucuses indicates that a presidential candidate is the front-runner. Although journalists certainly do not report stories without sources or evidence, they do not demand the weight of evidence or the strict standards of proof that statisticians and academic survey researchers (or judges) do. This fundamental difference is behind many of the problems associated with news media polling.

Reporters' preference for Type I instead of Type II errors is reinforced by the need for speed and the demand for novel and interesting stories. Statisticians would hesitate to claim something without a mass of convincing evidence; journalists often do not have the time to wait for such evidence to be gathered or the space to print it. But these pressures, especially speed, clash with the imperatives of survey research.

Differences in the way journalists and scholars interpret polls also stem from differences in the audiences they must satisfy. Journalists must appeal to members of the public who have few theories and little detailed knowledge about most subjects and expect events to be explained to them. Reporters therefore present compact, simplified pictures of the world. Complex stories riddled with caveats are not, in this context, newsworthy and not interesting to most people. The maxims of social science, however, require explanations that take into account all relevant factors and causes.

The statistician's response that an event is just random error, or the result of a complicated conjunction of causes or subject to "on the one hand, on the other" qualifications makes for dull copy. In presidential politics, for example, the machine-gun procession of primaries deals candidates ups and downs that demand explanation, and reporters duly write stories assigning causes for differences in performance that sometimes result merely from chance and luck.[4]

The course of events and the thirst for simple explanations sometimes lead to what might be called the variable of the month. In May a newspaper might publish a front page story about the controversy over legal abortion, replete with poll data indicating citizen interest. In June the lead story is about homelessness, and in July perhaps Central America. Although media pollsters may pick their survey topics from the headlines, the public may not have opinions on everything published on the front page. This sometimes leads to polls reporting vague notions masquerading as opinion.

The variable of the month leads to another problem. Attitudes toward abortion may not be reported in June and July, but this does not mean the subject has receded from public consciousness. Reports on the variable of the month often fail to suggest which issues have held people's attention for a long time and which have only a fleeting existence. Because the news media conduct polls only after an issue has become hot, they produce little trend data to differentiate abrupt changes in public opinion from longer-term patterns. But of course reporters are in the business of reporting news not "olds." Academic survey researchers, meanwhile, suffer from the opposite tendency. They are so wedded to repeating trend-revealing questions that they find it hard to add new ones to reflect changing political and social situations.

Often when practices are transplanted from one culture into another, underlying tensions emerge. Polls have been imported from academia into the newsroom and are now a staple of contemporary journalism. But the canons of survey research do not square easily with the canons of journalism. The clash between them means the potential for errors that is inherent in every poll is even greater in polls conducted and reported by news organizations.

Three Sources of Error

Statisticians identify three main sources of error in gathering and analyzing survey data: sampling error, measurement error, and specification error.

Sampling error is the most familiar threat to a poll's validity. Many reports based on polls mention a margin of error, usually plus or minus 3 percent, which is the error inherent in using interviews with 1,500 people to represent the opinions of several hundred million. Well-developed, standard statistical techniques can help limit this error to acceptable levels in most types of polls, if sometimes at heavy methodological and financial cost. But sampling error is not the only kind of error in selecting a sample, and other problems such as dwindling response rates are much more difficult to overcome.

Measurement error is the unintended effect on opinion of the questions themselves. Bad question design, or even a bad arrangement of good questions, can significantly bias survey results. Academic researchers have identified and controlled many measurement effects, and some media pollsters are aware of these advances. But the complexity of measurement problems remains a major source of error in the interpretation of polls.

Specification error, the most fundamental error, occurs when a theory is inappropriate for the opinion that the poll is trying to measure. Theories underlie all opinion polling and determine the form and content of the survey questions themselves. Media pollsters usually rely on simplistic and often unconscious theories. Unstated notions such as "most people have a single, unambiguous opinion on most issues that can be elicited with a few questions" are often implied in stories based on polls.

While most of the concern journalists express about errors in polls focuses on the sampling method, this should be the least of their worries. Although news organizations could certainly improve their sampling procedures, polls that do not measure what they seem to measure or that are used to prove or disprove poorly conceived theories are useless. Measurement and specification errors are the most serious perils of polling.

Sampling Error

All pollsters and many other people understand the basic principles behind random sampling.[5] Yet translating the relatively simple and clear need for a random sample of the population into an actual procedure for gathering poll respondents is far from easy. One sampling problem pollsters often gloss over is choosing a relevant population, or universe, of respondents. In national polls, this universe is usually all adult Americans. But in most preelection polling, for example, the intended universe includes only those likely to cast ballots, a population that pollsters spend considerable time and effort screening.

After deciding on a relevant population, pollsters must produce a representative sample. The theory of random sampling is elegant and simple, based on two rules and a mathematical theorem. The two rules are that everybody in the population of interest must have the same chance of being chosen for the sample ("equal chances") and that the chance of choosing each respondent must be independent of the chance of choosing another ("independent chances"). The mathematical theorem is the "law of large numbers," which implies that if these two rules are followed, then a poll of a large enough sample will usually yield results close to those from a census of the entire population.

When the first rule is followed, a large number of samples will give an unbiased picture of the population. It seems obvious that biases would result if some groups—rich people, white people, talkative people—were more likely to be included in a sample. When the second rule is followed as well, each new respondent within a sample will not be merely a carbon copy of the previous one. Through the law of large numbers and other mathematical theorems, mathematicians can make very precise statements about the character of samples when the two rules are followed. Specifically, they can predict the likelihood of various kinds of errors when inferences are made from the sample.

There is bound to be some discrepancy between the characteristics of the full population and the characteristics of smaller samples, and statistical sampling theory provides one way to estimate that sampling error— the famous "plus or minus three percent." Sampling error for presidential popularity, for example, provides an interval around the approval level that in nineteen out of twenty samples—if pollsters had the time, money, and patience to draw many more samples—would include the true value of what they are estimating. In 5 percent of the samples this interval would not include the true value.

The calculation to determine sampling error assumes a perfectly drawn sample. It does not reflect errors introduced by human fallibility that undermine the validity of standard statistical formulas. Specifically, it assumes a sample meets the assumptions of equal chances and independent chances. It provides no estimate of errors that can be caused by the many practical limitations and problems associated with achieving a good sample. And the calculation does not adjust for the errors that crop up in questionnaire design, interviewing, and analysis. But sampling error also does not cover the full range of problems connected with the sampling process per se. Furthermore, the practical problems of sampling—the difficulty of defining the underlying universe, getting people to agree to be interviewed, and obtaining a representative sample and avoiding selection bias—are particularly acute in news media polling.

DEFINING THE UNIVERSE. Despite their simplicity, the two rules of random sampling are hard to follow. Consider the equal chances rule. For telephone polls—by far the news media's favorite survey method— people with no phones (about 5 percent of households) have no chance of being interviewed, but those with multiple lines have multiple chances. Similarly, for at-home interviews, in which the sample is drawn by dwelling unit, people without homes have no chance of being interviewed and someone in a large household has less chance than someone in a small household.[6] The problem of multiple telephone lines is rather easy to solve: the interviewer simply ask respondents how many telephone lines they have and then weights the sample by dividing one by the number of lines. That is, someone with three lines counts only as one-third of a respondent, someone with two lines as one-half. Variations in household size are accounted for in much the same way. The pollster asks how many people live in the home, and weights the sample accordingly. But there is no simple way to include those without phones or homes. These people are simply missed. And because they are disproportionately poor, black or Hispanic, older, and rural, their exclusion introduces some upper-status bias into telephone samples.[7]

Even certain classes of people that have houses and telephones may be underrepresented for some methods of drawing samples. When interviewers randomly choose numbers from telephone directories, they miss people with unlisted numbers (often women or the elderly) and people who move often or who started telephone service after the directory was published. And pollsters sometimes identify households from voting lists that are incomplete or out of date.

Once a household is contacted, interviewers must be careful to choose at random an adult in the household. Otherwise, they are apt to speak to the person most likely to answer the door or the phone, usually a woman, or the person most readily available or most willing to cooperate. Pollsters ensure such randomness through various standard techniques, some more intrusive than others.[8]

RESPONSE RATES. Excluding people without telephones or houses is worrisome, but a far bigger problem for most surveys is refusals and nonresponse. In telephone surveys, for example, phone numbers are often generated through random-digit dialing, and there is no way of knowing whether the number is assigned to a person. Pollsters must often make many calls just to determine whether the number belongs to a person, a business, or no one.[9] Once the interviewer gets through to a household, other problems arise. The respondent asked for may refuse to participate—in which case a further call from a special interviewer known as a refusal converter is warranted—or may not be at home, so that a callback has to be arranged. Callbacks and attempts at refusal conversion are crucial in getting even a modest response.

Refusals and terminations of interviews can be significantly reduced if a skillful interviewer calls back or reschedules an interview. Most studies suggest permitting at least four calls per phone number. For example, a Canadian election survey conducted in 1988 required an average of 3.4 calls for each completed interview.[10] Having enough time to contact respondents is important. Half the interviews completed in the Canadian study were accomplished on the first day of calling, 16 percent on the second, 9 percent on the third, and 6 percent on the fourth. People who were difficult to interview differed in significant ways from those who were easy to get. Fifty-seven percent of the interviews completed on the first attempt were with women, even though only 50 percent of the respondents were female. Polls with few or no callbacks reach a disproportionate number of women and older adults, who are more likely to be at home when interviewers call. Samples become more representative with more callbacks.[11] This is why instant spot polls and the nightly tracking polls so popular with news organizations can yield unrepresentative samples: they require immediate turnaround, precluding callbacks.

Getting people to respond is becoming more difficult every year. In the biennial surveys conducted by the National Election Studies at the University of Michigan, refusal rates have climbed from 8 percent in the early 1950s to 25 percent.[12] In market research, one industry study found that refusal rates increased from 15 percent in 1982 to 34 percent in 1988. And answering machines now pose formidable difficulties for survey researchers.[13]

Potential errors caused by poor sampling or refusals can sometimes be partly corrected by weighting responses to reflect a given group's actual distribution in the population. This approach assumes, for instance, that poor people who respond are representative of all poor people. But the assumption seems unlikely: as John Brehm observed, "The respondent's decision to participate in surveys may share common factors with a citizen's decision to participate in politics." Reluctant respondents are less interested and involved in politics than amenable ones.[14]

As response rates dwindle, news media polls will be less successful than academic surveys in obtaining representative samples—academic surveys usually have more time and money at their disposal. To understand how much less successful, consider the results from the 1988 Canadian election survey. The survey shared several features with news media polls: interviewers conducted telephone surveys on each of the fifty days of the Canadian parliamentary campaign. Every day, a new random sample was drawn, with the goal of completing seventy to eighty interviews. Each sample was kept active as long as twelve days to complete

Table 4-1.   *Final Disposition for Telephone Numbers for Three Major News Media Polling Organizations, 1990–91* [a]

| | | Percent of total phone numbers known to be households | Percent of household sample | | | | |
| | | | Breakoffs and refusals | Callbacks not completed | No answer, answering machine, busy | Language barrier | Completed interviews |
Polling group	Number of polls						
X	2	63	24	11	19	6	40
Y	5	64	25	9	34	2	30
Z	11	67	21	7	18	3	52

Sources: Data provided by three unnamed polling organizations.

a. Because different polling organizations use different definitions for the disposition of numbers, it is difficult to make exact comparisons. Obtaining exact comparability would require extensive interviews with the field staff of each organization. We have not provided their names because we do not want to make unfair comparisons—especially since we cannot be sure that we have completely comparable data. All polls were completed in 1990 or 1991, and the number of completed interviews in each poll averaged 1,500. We thank the polling organizations that provided these data.

the interviews, so the time limitations were closer to those in a media poll than to the two or three months used by the typical academic survey. The study spent a lot of time and money to get a high response rate: the schedule allowed as many as fifteen callbacks for a phone number (although the average number of calls for each completed interview was 3.4), and a substantial effort was devoted to refusal conversion. Even so, only 57 to 60 percent of the residential numbers yielded completed interviews. The refusal rate was 31 percent. Another 9 percent of the phone numbers were scheduled for callbacks that could not be completed. Because many of the failed callbacks probably were tacit refusals, the actual refusal rate may have been closer to 40 percent.

For comparison, three major national news organizations have provided information about response rates for some telephone surveys they conducted in 1990 or 1991 that had key features in common. They used random-digit dialing or a variant, allowed about five days for interviewing, attempted callbacks on all the polls (two organizations stopped after four calls per phone number), and selected respondents within each household randomly according to who had the latest birthday or according to a more elaborate grid procedure. In short, the polls were conducted carefully and professionally. The organizations also used similar terms for the disposition of the numbers they called, but one must be careful about comparing results because the same terms can mean different things from one organization to another.

Two-thirds of the phone numbers were eligible households (table 4-1). The remaining third were mostly nonworking numbers, but also nonresidential numbers and households with no adult. Many numbers (18 to 34 percent) were classified as "no answer, answering machine, or busy." Some were undoubtedly nonhousehold numbers, but how many is unknown. To avoid the risk of inflating the response rate, they must be considered part of the household sample.

Between 20 and 25 percent of the people contacted either refused an interview or cut it short. An additional 7 to 11 percent scheduled callback interviews but did not go through with them, perhaps another form of noncooperation. Thus the total refusal rate was 28 to 35 percent. That is not much different from the results of the Canadian election study (31 percent outright refusals and 9 percent uncompleted callbacks). It is also not far from refusal rates of 15 to 38 percent reported for some commercial polls.[15]

The data in table 4-1—the most detailed accounting of response rates media pollsters have ever disclosed—are probably characteristic of the better media polls. What can be make of these results? Rates of completed interviews ranged from 30 to 52 percent, lower than those reported by news media pollsters in casual conversation, and not as good as many academic telephone surveys. The 1988 Super Tuesday study completed by the National Election Studies at the University of Michigan had a response rate of 62 percent. The rate of the 1988 Canadian election study was 57 to 60 percent.

But can media polls completed in about five days, with limited callbacks, limited refusal conversion in some cases, and only modest resources, do as well as academic surveys with much longer interviewing periods, many more callbacks, intensive refusal conversion, and much larger budgets? After all, only 78 percent of the completed interviews in the 1988 Canadian survey were finished after four calls. So if the Canadians had faced the same callback constraints as X, Y, and Z, their final response rate of (conservatively) 57 percent would have fallen to 44 percent, well within the range reported in table 4-1. Putting aside spot or instant polls, which report opinions within a day or two of an event and may have response rates 5 percent lower than the five-day polls described here, these national media polls appear to be doing satisfactorily, given their extraordinary time pressures and limited funding.[16]

Clearly, however, the variability in completion rates is worrisome and requires further examination.[17] Unfortunately, no one knows precisely at what point completion rates begin to introduce serious biases into survey research—is it 90 percent; 80 percent; 50 percent; 40 percent? We would be surprised, however, if rates of 30 percent yielded representative samples of the population. If close scrutiny reveals that samples with low completion rates seriously underrepresent older, less affluent, less educated, or minority populations, then adjustments cannot be made with mathematical weights. But without knowing the extent or consequences of such bias, one cannot assess the costs and benefits of investing more time and money to complete a survey.[18]

SAMPLING PROBLEMS IN 1992.   Two sampling problems that occurred with media polls in 1992 illustrate the special difficulties that arise when news organizations conduct and report opinion surveys. The first occurred a month before the New Hampshire primary. Following President Bush's 1992 State of the Union message on January 28, CBS News aired a program that invited viewers to use an 800 number to register their views on a few questions about the speech. In conjunction with the call-in, a separate sample of 1,241 adults interviewed earlier in January were reinterviewed that night after the speech.

News organizations have recently grown fond of call-in "polls" using 800 or 900 numbers. These unscientific pseudo-polls, with self-selected, unrepresentative samples, have been roundly discredited by academic survey researchers. They are the junk bonds of the polling business. Yet they persist.

CBS had intended to draw a clear distinction between the unscientific call-in responses and the scientific poll results: the call-in was simply a way to increase viewer involvement. But viewers understandably found it difficult to distinguish between the two sources of information. The confusion was further aggravated by the side-by-side presentation of the poll and the call-in and by on-air commentary that continually blurred the distinction between the two.[19] Episodes like this undermine the credibility of serious survey research and cause pollsters to wonder whether Gresham's law of money might be paraphrased, "bad polls drive good polls out of circulation."

Another 1992 sampling error occurred during the New Hampshire Republican primary, when an exit poll conducted by Voter Research & Surveys (VRS) predicted George Bush would defeat Pat Buchanan by 6 percentage points.[20] In fact, Bush beat Buchanan by 16 points, 53 percent to 37 percent.

What went wrong? VRS conducted interviews in only 60 precincts, but the error probably was not caused by covering too few polling sites. More likely, respondents within each precinct were not selected properly.[21] Women—who were more likely than men to support Bush—may have been less willing to participate. The authors of the poll, however, believed that zealous Buchanan voters were more eager than the less motivated Bush voters to fill out exit poll questionnaires and "send a message."[22]

Whatever the source of error, its impact was magnified because it was a news media poll. Bush's New Hampshire victory was actually solid— much greater than Lyndon Johnson's over Eugene McCarthy, Gerald Ford's over Ronald Reagan, or Jimmy Carter's over Ted Kennedy. Yet the story the public read and heard just after the primary was far more favorable to Buchanan than it should have been and gave his campaign valuable momentum at the outset of the primaries.

DISCLOSURE OF SAMPLING INFORMATION. Although accurate sampling entails a complicated methodology, the news media do a mediocre job of explaining to the public what affects accuracy. To be sure, some news organizations employ reasonably high standards for disclosing methodological information. The *Washington Post Deskbook on Style* suggests,

> The more important the results of a poll are to a story, the more technical information must be given about the survey data. A casual or general reference, such as *Recent polls in several states show strong support for the farm bill* requires no elaboration. But when the poll itself is the story, details are essential. . . . The story must give the identity of the poll's sponsor, the dates it was taken, the number of persons interviewed and their characteristics (registered voters, employed, Catholics etc.), the method of polling (telephone, in person, etc.) and the margin of sampling error.[23]

CBS News has somewhat stricter standards for casual mention of polls but similar standards for major stories. Casual mentions of a poll should identify the organization conducting the poll, or the poll's sponsor if it is a special interest group, and the dates of the interviewing. Major stories must also describe the population sample (nationwide, statewide, and so forth) and state the margin of error.[24]

Most news organizations take a more casual approach. We reviewed all references to polls, except sports polls, in the *Chicago Tribune* from July 1, 1988, to December 31, 1989, to learn how polls were reported by a typical local newspaper. We studied July 1988 to December 1989

Table 4-2. *Reports of Sampling Method in All* Chicago Tribune
Articles Based on Polls, July 1, 1988–December 31, 1989
Percent (numbers of articles in parentheses)

Information provided	All poll articles	Articles on media polls not conducted by the Tribune	Tribune poll articles
Poll sponsor	94 (115)	100 (60)	100 (28)
Dates of survey	34 (42)	53 (32)	89 (25)
Sample size	66 (80)	63 (38)	89 (25)
Population	48 (59)	55 (33)	89 (25)
Method	34 (42)	42 (25)	64 (18)
Sampling error	32 (39)	52 (31)	86 (24)
Subgroup error margins	16 (20)	33 (20)	71 (20)
Response rates	0 (0)	0 (0)	0 (0)
Total number of polls	122	60	28

Source: Authors' calculations.

because it covered a presidential campaign and the Chicago mayoral primary and general election.

The quality of reporting methodology improved as the focus narrowed from all poll-based articles to media poll articles to reports on *Tribune* polls. This is mostly because reports on *Tribune* polls were treated as major stories, and there was often a separate box discussing their technical aspects.

Although poll sponsors were identified in 94 percent of the articles, only half the stories mentioned survey dates, sample size, population sampled, method of administration (telephone or in-person), or sampling error (table 4-2).[25] A third of the media poll stories noted that the sampling error for subgroups was larger than the overall sampling error, and 71 percent of the *Chicago Tribune* stories mentioned this. As in the media generally, none of the stories mentioned response rates. Thus the *Tribune's* reporting of poll methodology sometimes provided a great deal of detail and sometimes too little.

Why so little information on the details of polls in half the media poll reports? Space limitations may have precluded fuller descriptions. Long articles were twice as likely as others to report the sampling error, but the *Tribune* polls were normally reported in longer articles. Whatever the reason for the deficiencies, reporters and editors need to work harder at providing adequate descriptions of polls.

The statement that a poll "has a margin of error of plus or minus 4 percent," as the *Boston Globe* typically puts it, or that "in theory, in 19 cases out of 20, the results based on such samples will differ by no more than 3 percentage points in either direction from what would have been obtained by seeking out all American adults," as the *New York Times* more accurately intones, says nothing about the practical problems of sampling. Sampling error is just the tip of the iceberg. Properly defining the underlying universe, achieving an acceptable response rate, reducing selection bias—these are the formidable problems. Of course, media pollsters must report sampling error to the public. But by focusing attention on this tiny source of error, they convey a specious precision (a problem aggravated by referring to sampling error as "*the* margin of error" as the *Boston Globe* does). The far greater challenge is to properly assess and address the other, more serious threats to validity.

Measurement Error

Measurement and specification errors, as we shall see, are often five or ten times greater than sampling error. They are more troubling even than such practical sampling problems as decreasing response rates. Although practical sampling problems might compromise news media polling, measurement and specification errors definitely do. And errors caused by mistakes in measurement and specification are harder to understand and measure. Finally, although pollsters can solve sampling problems (increase callbacks, expand the interviewing period), antidotes to measurement and specification error lie less in the realm of science than the realm of craftsmanship.

There is the story of the three baseball umpires who are talking about the way they call balls and strikes. The first umpire says, "Some are balls and some are strikes, and I call 'em like I see 'em." The second says, "Some are balls and some are strikes, and I call 'em like they is." The third says, "Some are balls and some are strikes, and they ain't nothin' till I call 'em."

Likewise, measurement in polling means pinning numbers on intangibles—hopes and fears, likes and dislikes, perceptions and intentions. Measurement error comes from asking questions that do not generate appropriate responses. It is like using a ruler that you think is 12 inches long but is really only 11.[26] The effect of measurement error on the quality and usefulness of data potentially dwarfs the sampling error of even the smallest subgroups.

QUESTION WORDING. The most watched presidential popularity polls have been conducted by the Gallup and Harris organizations.[27]

These companies use different questions to assess presidential popularity. Harris asks, "How would you rate the job [name] is doing as president? Would you say that he is doing an excellent, pretty good, only fair, or a poor job?" Harris lumps all the "only fair" and "poor" responses into a single negative category. Gallup asks, "Do you approve or disapprove of the way [name] is handling his job as president?" The results of the two surveys often differ widely.

In January 1978 the *Washington Post* asked the Harris and the Gallup popularity questions in the same poll. In response to the Gallup question, 63 percent said they approved of President Jimmy Carter's handling of the presidency. Answering the Harris question, 48 percent of the same respondents said Carter was "excellent" or "pretty good." The difference of 15 percentage points, a product of measurement error, far outweighed the polls' 3 percent statistical sampling error. A cross-tabulation found that of the 40 percent who had answered "only fair" to the Harris question, 46 percent approved of the president's performance and 45 percent disapproved according to the Gallup question. For roughly half the respondents, "only fair" meant approval; for the other half, it meant disapproval. The Harris question simply does not clearly elicit positive or negative sentiment because "only fair" is so ambiguous.

The *Post* then elaborated on the experiment, asking respondents to grade Carter's handling of his job as A, B, C, D, or F. Overall, more than a third gave him a C, an expression of ambivalence or indecision captured by neither the Harris or Gallup questions. Of those who answered "only fair" to the Harris question, 20 percent gave Carter an A or B, an equal number gave him a D or F, and more than half, 55 percent, gave him a C. When responses to the Gallup question were compared to the *Post* grading scale, the mildly approving or disapproving answers also revealed little conviction. While the Harris formulation is ambiguous and the Gallup question compels too much outright approval or disapproval, the *Post* question is also imperfect. Some of the C response in 1978 probably reflected a feeling that the president had done a mediocre job and some merely reflected uncertainty.

Two polls on American attitudes toward U.S.-Soviet relations that were conducted in June 1978 provide another illustration that the way questions are worded and the choice of answers offered profoundly affects the opinions they elicit. A Harris poll asked a nationwide sample of Americans, "Do you favor or oppose détente—that is, the United States and Russia seeking out areas of agreement and cooperation?" Seventy-one percent said they favored détente and only 15 percent reported that they opposed it. The same month the *New York Times* and CBS News asked, "Should the United States try harder to relax tension with the Soviet Union or should it get tougher in its dealings with the Russians?" Thirty percent said they thought the United States should relax tensions; 53 percent favored getting tougher. Did Americans favor or oppose U.S.-Soviet détente in June 1978? The *Times* claimed that "close to twice as many in the survey said they wanted a policy that would 'get tough' with the Soviet Union as preferred greater efforts to relax tensions," while the Harris survey said "reports that Americans have become less favorable toward detente . . . simply have no basis in fact. To the contrary, there appear to be sizable majorities of the public who deeply hope that agreements between the world's two leading superpowers can be achieved." Again, the difference is attributable to the different wording in the two polls.[28] Value-laden phrases, "seeking out areas of agreement and cooperation" in one poll and "get tough" in the other, strongly attracted the support of respondents.

Similarly, in the 1960s public opinion toward the Vietnam War was reported as hawkish or dovish depending on the wording of the survey questions. If a question associated negative terms with withdrawal from the war ("defeat," "Communist takeover," "loss of American credibility"), the public sounded hawkish. But when negative terms were associated with a pro-war position ("killings," "continuing the war," "domestic disruptions"), it sounded dovish.[29]

News organizations and other pollsters could avoid the most egregious measurement errors if they familiarized themselves with the many methodological studies on problems of question wording.[30] These studies show, for example, that questions in which alternative answers are posed in a balanced way ("Should the government see to it that everyone receives adequate heath care, or should everyone be responsible for their own health care?") are preferable to the one-sided, agree-disagree questions that are so tempting to time-conscious pollsters ("Do you agree or disagree that the government should see to it that everyone receives adequate health care?").

Most experts believe that poll questions should offer a middle choice ("Are things getting better, worse, or staying about the same?"). Some, however, disagree because respondents often seek refuge in the middle to avoid revealing their true views. But the more carefully the pollsters are prepared to analyze the middle option response, the stronger the case for including a middle choice. Similarly, there is some dispute over whether questions should explicitly offer respondents the "don't know" option or whether that should remain a volunteered response. Most researchers agree that the answer depends on the kind of opinion being solicited. These are two instances in which there is no cookbook guide to correct wording so much as an inventory of alternatives and a discussion of their consequences.

Experts also warn about the inadequacies of questions that have "normatively correct" answers ("Did you vote?" "Are you racially prejudiced?"). One such norm for most Americans is discomfort with the outright banning of anything—guns, abortions, unpopular speech. In a poll conducted in Detroit in 1976, half the sample was asked, "Do you think the United States should allow public speeches in favor of communism?" and the other half was asked, "Do you think the United States should forbid public speeches in favor of communism?" Fifty-six percent replied that such speeches should not be allowed, but only 39 percent said they should be forbidden.[31]

Pollsters must also phrase questions in specific terms. Instead of asking whether people go to art museums often, seldom, or never, it is better to ask whether they go twice a year, once a year, once every two years, and so on. An even better wording would be, "How many times did you go to an art museum last year?" The most common mistakes are questions with indefinite antecedents, overlapping alternatives, false premises, and double negatives; questions that pose two or more questions in one; questions that are emotionally charged, embarrassing, or overly technical.[32]

ATTITUDES AND NONATTITUDES. Another common form of error stems from attempting to measure attitudes that do not exist. Few pollsters would deny that many people have no opinions on issues that concern politicians and journalists. A poll sample that includes responses from many people with no adequate knowledge or no opinion, or both, will be inaccurate. Observers disagree, however, on how prevalent these nonattitudes are in polls and how serious their effect on results.

The controversy began with a disturbing article by Philip Converse that examined whether the public organizes its political opinions along ideologically liberal and conservative lines.[33] According to Converse, few people can even explain the terms liberalism and conservatism, and fewer still have attitudes shaped by their liberal or conservative identification. Most people's attitudes on one issue seem completely unrelated to their views on others. Even views on a single issue can appear random. Using panel data from the same respondents (a 1956 sample reinterviewed in 1958 and 1960), Converse discovered that fewer than two-thirds expressed the same attitudes on a particular issue that they had expressed in the previous surveys. We would expect that by chance one-half would have picked the same answer twice. He suggested that many people had no firm opinions on issues, and they simply picked among the answers at random.

From these and other results, Converse drew disheartening conclusions. Most people know and care little about most political issues. Ideology is confined to a very few. Many people make up random answers to survey questions when asked about issues they are not familiar with or interested in. That nonattitudes are rampant in survey responses calls into question the validity, reliability, and meaning of public opinion calls.

Not all these conclusions have stood up to scrutiny. Analysts generally agree that Americans "morselize" their political beliefs, rarely following the ideologies recognized by elites or connecting views on one subject with those on another. For example, most people favor lower taxes yet also want more and better public services.[34] But nonattitudes are not so pervasive, and they may often be the result of faulty questions, not the ignorance, caprice, or indifference of respondents. Clear political attitudes and ideologies are more common than Converse supposes. When one study tested the measurement error of survey questions against conventional predictors of ideological consistency and attitude holding such as education, income, and political engagement and activity, it found little variation.[35] Measurement error was widespread. The questionnaires themselves were sometimes vague and unable reliably to reflect actual opinions. People also seem to have unstable and changeable attitudes, but once corrections are made for measurement error in the questions, it is common to find people who care a great deal about some matters—sometimes the vast majority of respondents. As two social scientists have said: "There are some authentic opinions, tenaciously held, and some nonattitudes, casually expressed. There are patches of knowledge and expanses of ignorance."[36]

The connection between the prevalence of nonattitudes and measurement errors in polls should be apparent. It is very easy to ask questions that make sense to a reporter knowledgeable about a subject, and it is equally easy for respondents to provide answers even though they know virtually nothing about the topic. Foreign policy issues are a gold mine of nonattitudes. Asked if they favor or oppose multinational aid to Surinam, many Americans will obligingly provide an answer, even though they would be hard pressed to locate the country on a map or to describe what sort of aid it might require. The expression of nonattitudes is also susceptible to small variations in the wording and ordering of questions and other measurement conditions. Although it is difficult to know how much error nonattitudes add to a poll, a necessary first step is to differentiate nonattitudes from definite attitudes. Attitudes based on extensive knowledge and careful thought are more stable and deeply held than those based on skimpy impressions or even worse on information supplied in a poll itself. Polls taken more than a few months before an election campaign register little beyond name recognition, and the survey results may change quickly as voters come to know the candidates better.[37] This accounts for the supposed battles between dark horses and front runners that constitute most of modern television election coverage.

The 1988 presidential election illustrates the effects of early preelection polling on people's expectations of candidates and perceptions of their performance. After his defeat, Michael Dukakis was accused of blowing his 17-point lead over George Bush in the polls after the summer Democratic convention. But Dukakis's lead in July was much smaller than the raw numbers indicated because most people still did not know much about him. Democratic primary voters had started out knowing "almost nothing" about Michael Dukakis, and they knew only "a little" by Super Tuesday on March 8 (figure 4-1).[38] Much of what people did know resulted from the candidate's third-place showing in the Iowa caucuses and his victory in New Hampshire. Even after his campaign blitzes on television in the Super Tuesday states, the electorate still knew far less about Dukakis than about Gary Hart, Jesse Jackson, or George Bush, although they did know more about him than about the hapless Bruce Babbitt, who fell from view after his poor showing in Iowa. So, Dukakis's strong showing in some Super Tuesday states was based on rather meager knowledge about him.

A similar lack of familiarity probably accounted for his 17-point advantage over Bush in July. Dukakis's "lost" lead was created by pollsters who equated the value of July's poll results with the value of soundings taken late in October. They assumed that voters were equally familiar with both candidates and were continually assessing them. But in the dead of summer the election was three months away. It was mostly on the minds of reporters, pollsters, politicians, pundits, and political junkies. Dukakis was thus helped by his status as a virtual unknown, while Bush, for better and worse, was well known. The early summer polls did

Figure 4-1. *Public Knowledge of Candidates before Super Tuesday, 1988*

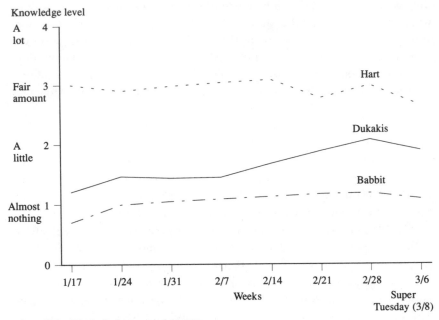

Source: National Election Studies surveys in sixteen states.

Bush, for better and worse, was well known. The early summer polls did measure something—perhaps the news media attention accorded to the Democratic convention—but they were a poor predictor of the November election.

CHANGEABILITY OF OPINION. Nonattitudes are not the only problem with accepting polling data at face value. Attitudes and beliefs also change. In the 1984 presidential campaign, people's impressions of the less well known candidates shifted dramatically during the primaries and stabilized only when the campaigns were nearly finished.[39] The newcomers, John Glenn, Gary Hart, and Jesse Jackson, emerged from the primaries with images just about as stable as those of Walter Mondale and Ronald Reagan, who were already well known before the campaign began.

But if people do learn about candidates during campaigns, they learn slowly. So early poll reports may seize upon ill-formed and fleeting images that will be quickly overturned. In the 1992 Democratic presidential primary campaign in Florida, reporters' lack of vigilance about the volatility of preelection polls led to some poor news coverage and questionable interpretations of results. Most reports during the final ten days of the campaign described the race between Governor Bill Clinton and former Senator Paul Tsongas as "neck and neck" and "too close to call." The expectation of a tight race was based on two polls, one commissioned by the Florida newspapers owned by the New York Times Company and one by Mason-Dixon Political Media Research. But both were conducted at least ten days before the election. In the meantime, Clinton had won overwhelmingly in Georgia and Senators Bob Kerrey and Tom Harkin had dropped out of the race. In short, the news assessments were based on obsolete data.

Not only were the two polls out of date, but they showed that nearly a third of the voters had not yet made up their minds. Despite all that— and despite the upsurge in campaigning that could be expected a few days before the election—reporters allowed their expectations and the tone of their coverage to be shaped by these polls, maybe because they needed some drama, excitement, and uncertainty in an otherwise dull Super Tuesday. The Clinton campaign, whose private polls apparently showed that Clinton had pulled substantially ahead in the last week, did nothing to dispel the perception created by the press that the race was tight. The final tally showed Clinton with 51 percent of the vote and Tsongas with 35 percent. The defeat was all the more crushing for Tsongas when press post mortems portrayed Clinton's victory as an unexpected impressive triumph.[40]

Thus in addition to sampling problems—the difficulty of correctly identifying eventual voters in the sample—preelection polls suffer from an exceedingly short life span as voters learn more about the candidates and are swayed by daily reports.

An analysis of every poll of the 1988 electoral season has shown that variations in poll results consisted of two parts: intrinsic volatility in preferences for the candidates and variability from sampling error. Six months before the general election there was a 3 percent to 5 percent net change, or volatility, in voters' preferences from one poll to the next. By election day, opinions had finally crystallized, and almost all the variability was due to sampling error. Before the settling out, preelection poll data are capricious and not very meaningful. Journalists should thus report at least two figures when they discuss early election polls–the standard sampling error and a figure for pure volatility of the electorate.[41] A good example of this kind of journalism appeared in a *Chicago Tribune* article, "Simon Leading Martin, But It's Not Set in Stone," on the 1990 U.S. Senate race in Illinois. The opening paragraph made clear the volatility of early polls:

"Senator Paul Simon holds a big lead over his Republican challenger, Rep. Lynn Martin, but the edge is not decisive by any means, and Martin can hope to close the gap as she becomes better known, a new *Tribune* poll shows." The article went on to discuss how their difference in support depended on the electorate's knowledge of them.[42]

How can pollsters ensure that preelection surveys are measuring solid views and not fickle impressions? Early in a campaign, respondents may hold and express real attitudes, but these are based on little thought and information and are thus likely to change as the campaign progresses. Early preelection polls should therefore include indicators of knowledge and interest. If these two measures are low, poll reports should carry prominent warnings that change is likely, as the *Tribune*'s article did. In an ideal world, pollsters would refrain from taking early preelection polls seriously and would avoid using them to set unrealistic standards for candidates to uphold.

THE CONTEXT OF QUESTIONS. The context in which a survey question is asked can pose another obstacle to measuring attitudes. Previous questions in the survey may influence answers by suggesting a framework for deciding what the current question is about. They may make certain responses sound redundant or implicitly pressure respondents to choose answers that conform to their earlier responses. For example, a question on a respondent's attitude toward abortion that was preceded by questions about religion, traditional values, and the sanctity of life would probably get a response different from one to the same question preceded by questions about rape, women's rights, and government interference in private life. If a respondent says that life is sacred or that government should stay out of private decisions, the consistency effect could lead him or her to answer the abortion question in a manner consistent with previous answers.

Another example is the placement of the question on whether the respondent approves of the way the president is doing his job. During the Reagan presidency, pollsters noted that when the approval question was placed at the beginning of the survey, it elicited a more positive response than when it was placed near the end, after many questions about the state of the economy, foreign policy, and other matters. Apparently, most people liked Reagan but were not always so pleased with his policies or programs.

In the spring and summer of 1992 much of the variability from poll to poll in the public's support for the presidential candidates stemmed from differences in the order of asking questions. For example, the *New York Times*/CBS News poll consistently reported lower numbers for H. Ross Perot. That was partly because it asked respondents to rate the candidates before soliciting their candidate choice. Some people who first said that they did not know enough about Perot to rate him were inhibited from saying that they would vote for him. The *Time*/CNN poll regularly reported the least support for President Bush, probably because before asking people for their vote choice the poll asked them "How well do you think things are going in the country these days?," which yielded many negative responses and sour feelings about the incumbent. Not surprisingly, polls conducted for *Newsweek, USA Today*, and the Times-Mirror Center for the People and the Press found that Perot did better when voters were first asked to choose between George Bush and Bill Clinton, and then asked whom they preferred in a three-way race, than he did when voters were presented with a three-way choice initially.[43]

Answering a survey question is a complex process.[44] People create responses to questions, not by conjuring them from nothing but by using available materials to put together a reasonable answer. They do not concoct responses so much as construct them. Confronted with confusing or irrelevant questions, they will use clues from previous questions—and from the interviewer— to build an answer.

SOME CORRECTIVES. The more one explores the many sources of measurement error, the more hopeless the prospect seems of ever preparing a poll questionnaire that is not fatally flawed. Nevertheless, three strategies for battling such errors have proved helpful.

First, pollsters must acknowledge that attitudes on most social and political matters are complex, often ambiguous, and occasionally contradictory. A single question simply cannot capture opinion. Valid interpretation of the public's views on even one issue requires questions with different formats and alternative wordings. Although this may seem strange, it is the norm in other disciplines. Economists, for example, have long relied on an assortment of indicators and composite indexes for appraising economic performance. Public opinion is far more elusive than economic performance. Yet ironically, cost-and time-conscious media pollsters avoid using multiple indicators. To limit measurement error, they must use many different gauges of opinion.

Measurement error can also be reduced by using split-sample experiments that examine the effects of alternative question wordings, as the

1988 Canadian election study did. The free trade agreement with the United States was hotly debated in the 1988 Canadian parliamentary campaign. Half the poll respondents were asked whether they supported the "free trade agreement that Canada had reached with the United States." For the other half "the Mulroney government" was substituted for "Canada." Early in the campaign, the first question produced 12 points more support than the second. This difference eroded as the campaign drew on, probably because voters gradually came to informed opinions and became less susceptible to changes in question wording. The Conservative party countercampaign, which stressed Mulroney's competence and character, may also have neutralized the negative connotations of the "Mulroney" question. Such experimental techniques can help determine whether public attitudes are strong or weak, crystallized or unfocused. If minor wording changes produce large variations in opinion, many respondents are open to fairly gentle persuasion on the relevant question. These experiments also shed light on how the public makes its decisions. (If reporters base stories on split-sample and other experimental techniques, they should alert their readers and viewers whenever the wording of questions makes a significant difference in expressed opinions.)

Finally, media pollsters will make great progress in combating measurement error—particularly the confusion of nonattitudes with clear ones—if they incorporate more questions that probe the prominence of various issues to the public. Salience is tied to measurement error, but it is also closely bound to another source of inaccuracies in polling: specification error.

Specification Error

If measurement error results from using a ruler shorter than one thinks it is, specification error comes from trying to gauge the length of an object by weighing it. A constant bane of journalistic polls, specification error arises when sample selection, questionnaire construction, and data analysis are guided by defective underlying theories and assumptions.

It might seem odd to speak of theories and journalism in the same breath. Journalists might claim that theories and complicated models are for professors. Media pollsters simply measure and report the public's opinion; they do not test theories. Indeed, journalists might say that using theories to guide the way they design, conduct, and analyze polls would contravene a crucial tenet of their craft: objectivity. But in fact, news media polls, like any type of investigation, are beset by implicit or unspecified theories. Because the theories are not subject to criticism and debate, they have a decisive but hidden influence on the questions pollsters ask and how they interpret the answers.

SALIENCE. One implicit assumption underlying most public opinion research is that people's minds are like filing cabinets—that they contain clear opinions on many discrete topics and group them into categories, like memos tucked away in file folders. To find the public's opinion on whether the federal deficit is out of control, for instance, the pollster simply pulls the file marked "economy," locates the memo marked "deficit, federal," and reads it. The method assumes that the public's opinion of the deficit, or of any other matter, can be ascertained by writing a question that will efficiently pick the correct file and disclose its contents.

But most people do not have clear, crystallized attitudes on every issue. And the attitudes they do have are not necessarily organized by issue or retrievable by topic. Instead, people cluster in a few "issue publics."[45] That is, people generally have a few issues that are particularly important to them and to which their political antennae are attuned. Only a small cadre of political elites think about a great many political issues and try to maintain ideological consistency. Other people have a limited appetite for political matters and are not burdened by an urge for consistency.

How a pollster conceives of the way people organize their views—if you will, the pollster's theory of public opinion—determines the kinds of questions asked. Specification and measurement are inextricably intertwined. Foolish questions are usually the result of both faulty measurement and faulty assumptions. Bad theories, such as phrenology, lead to useless measurements—counting the number of bumps on people's heads. Polls based on the filing-cabinet model inevitably produce error-prone results that can vary widely with seemingly minor changes in question wording. Instead of asking anyone about anything, pollsters should target questions to people with definite attitudes on a particular topic. Otherwise the answers will be unreliable or even invalid.

The results from an unpublished poll conducted in a Boston suburb illustrate the need for incorporating questions that establish salience. Asked questions about their attitudes toward compulsory school busing, the poll indicated that the community supported the policy. But the poll also included several questions to determine how important the issue was to each respondent. (One of the most powerful questions was simply whether the household included any school-age children.) Those who thought busing was an important subject were strongly opposed to it.

Pollsters in general and news media pollsters in particular place far too much emphasis on whether people favor or oppose a particular policy and far too little on salience. But they do so at the risk of distorting their findings.[46] Polls should include many questions about whether people follow particular issues closely, how interested they are in them, and how much they know about them. Because of severe limitations on time and space, news media pollsters will be reluctant to make this change; more questions on salience would mean that polls would cover fewer topics. However, polls would be better for having less breadth and more depth.

SPECIFICATION, ISSUES, AND VOTING. Changes in theories of why people vote the way they do also illustrate the ways different assumptions and theories affect the kinds of questions asked in surveys. Early studies of voting behavior assumed that a voter's decision was determined by social and economic characteristics—religion, occupation, urban or rural residency.[47] Accordingly, pollsters who—explicitly or implicitly—subscribed to that model asked many personal background and demographic questions but few of the questions on issues that have become standard fare today. Refinements to this simple theory have yielded a succession of new voting models, each giving rise to new survey questions. For example, a more sophisticated psychologically based model that linked voting patterns to long-term partisan attachment introduced questions on party identification.[48] Subsequent studies that pointed to the importance of public preferences on policy issues also influenced questionnaires.[49]

Voting models determine not only the questions asked but ultimately the answers. At the height of U.S. engagement in Vietnam, some political scientists concluded that Vietnam policy had almost no effect on voting in the 1968 election, pointing to survey data showing little correlation between people's support for withdrawal or escalation and the way they cast their ballots.[50] But the assumption that attitudes toward Vietnam policy could be summed up by whether people were hawks or doves was flawed. Voting was strongly correlated with other attitudes, in particular whether people thought the war was a mistake or how well they thought the Johnson administration had handled it.[51] A more subtle theory of reactions to political issues would have led the political scientists to a different conclusion.

On any issue, public opinion usually manifests itself in at least three ways. First, people may think about it in terms of position, where they stand ideologically (hawk or dove, pro-life or pro-choice) when confronted with policy alternatives. When journalists or political observers comment on issues, most think in terms of position, and questions in polls are expressed accordingly. But people may also consider the same subject in terms of valence. Instead of eliciting a Left or Right response, valence matters are those on which everyone agrees—the desirability of peace and prosperity, the deplorability of political corruption—and people think of them in terms of politicians or organizations identified with those values.[52] Finally, attitudes on a particular issue may reflect a concern for performance, the way the matter has been handled or is likely to be handled. On most important political issues, people typically hold all three kinds of views simultaneously. On America's intervention in Vietnam a person might have been a hawk or a dove, have regarded either the Democrats or the Republicans as the party of peace, and have felt that Lyndon Johnson had, from a purely administrative standpoint, done a good or bad job of handling the war.

This three-part theory of perception can help explain, for instance, public opinion on abortion. One way to account for the differences in poll results is to consider the effects of measurement error. Differently worded questions elicit different answers. So Americans tend to oppose abortions when asked whether they should be permitted in situations other than rape, incest, or when the health of the mother is endangered, but they tend to tolerate abortions when asked whether the government should have the right to prohibit them.

Another way to think about these apparent discrepancies is in terms of specification error. If people think about issues not only in terms of their position but simultaneously in terms of valence, polls should reach different conclusions according to the type of issue implicit in the wording of the questions. When a question frames abortion as a position issue to discover the public's ideological attitudes about policy alternatives (that is, under what circumstances abortion should be legal), the public either is divided or tilts toward prohibiting it.

But when a question couches the issue in certain valence terms, tapping such traditional American values as individualism and liberty (Should a woman be allowed to decide whether to have an abortion?), opinion takes on a more liberal cast. Questions concerning abortion are framed rarely in terms of performance (Do you approve or disapprove of the way candidate A or public official B is reacting to the abortion issue?) but are hotly debated in position or valence terms.

Distinguishing between abortion as a position issue or a valence issue is not just an academic exercise. Liberal organizations such as the National Abortion Rights Action League and the National Organization for Women have tried to frame the debate less as an argument over policy options than as an argument over who should decide—that is, a matter of freedom of choice. Such groups realize that defining abortion as a valence issue is more likely to garner support for their point of view.

This three-part theory of the ways issues are perceived may be right or wrong. But armed with this specification of how people think about issues, a pollster would ask a certain line of questions and do a certain kind of analysis. A different model would lead the pollster down an entirely different path.

SPECIFICATION, RACE, AND POLLS.   Theories help interpret polls. A poll of attitudes toward busing for school desegregation, for example, might find that many white people oppose busing. Does this mean that the white electorate is racist? Or does it mean that busing is simply a bad idea? What about affirmative action? Is white opposition the consequence of racism? To answer these questions, analysts must specify what constitutes racism.

Opposition to affirmative action may be based on racism, but it may also be a principled rejection of the idea that anyone should be hired on criteria other than merit. Interpreting public attitudes toward affirmative action requires a better understanding of racism. If racism can be straight-forwardly measured by a respondent's like or dislike of blacks, then the idea that opposition to affirmative action is racially motivated might be tested by simply seeing if dislike of blacks is related to rejection of affirmative action. Yet there are many reasons to suspect that racism cannot be so easily measured. So researchers have invented more subtle ways of detecting it, including changes in question wording in which a random half of respondents are asked their opinion of affirmative action for blacks and another random half are asked about affirmative action for other groups.[53] This allows researchers to distinguish opposition based upon dislike of the group from opposition based upon disapproval of the program itself. Both factors seem at work in white objections to affirmative action and other racially sensitive policies.

Even this stratagem, however, must contend with theoretical difficulties. Some researchers claim that there is a new form of racism, symbolic racism, that rests on the principle that rewards should be based on hard work and the stereotype that blacks are less hard working than other Americans. This, it is claimed, leads to rhetoric about merit and achievement that is a disguised form of racism.[54] Opposition to affirmative action, then, might appear to be based on allegiance to meritocratic principles rather than on old-fashioned avowals of black inferiority, when in fact it is an expression of racism. The debate over the nature and extent of symbolic racism and its relationship to old-style racism demonstrates the difficulty of interpreting opinions about policy matters involving a racial element.[55] Depending on one's theory of racism, opposition to affirmative action may or may not be racist. In this case, as in many others, the polls do not speak for themselves. To interpret them, one must have some theory of what constitutes racism.

Specification problems also inhibit the interpretation of polls involving black candidates. In the 1982 California governor's race the black mayor of Los Angeles, Tom Bradley, won 48.1 percent of the vote and was narrowly defeated by former California Attorney General George Deukmejian with 49.3 percent. All of the nineteen published polls had indicated Bradley would win, although they had shown his lead ebbing from an average of 12 percentage points between August 1981 and October 1982 to 4 points two weeks before the election, with 12 percent undecided.[56] Polls on contests involving other black candidates have also performed badly in predicting election winners. Although polls in the 1989 Virginia gubernatorial election showed black Lieutenant Governor Douglas Wilder leading white Attorney General Marshall Coleman by an average of 7 percentage points (with 10 percent of the voters undecided), Wilder won by only 51.1 percent to 49.8 percent.[57] Similarly, in the 1989 New York mayoral campaign, black Manhattan Borough President David Dinkins led U.S. Attorney Rudolf Giuliani by an average of 14 points yet beat him only 50 percent to 48 percent.[58]

Even though these two black candidates won, they were still subject to "the Bradley effect," the tendency of polls to overestimate black candidates' share of the vote. A more accurate estimate of the outcome in an interracial election may be made by assuming that the entire percentage of undecided voters in the final survey will vote against the minority candidate.[59] The rationale is that people do not want to tell a pollster they are voting against the minority candidate, so they describe themselves as undecided or even as supporters of the minority candidate. This explanation assumes that racists are unwilling to admit their racism to a pollster, and it squares with the theory of symbolic racism.[60]

This explanation of the Bradley effect may be correct, but it requires accepting that racism has become hidden and implicit, a hotly debated theory. There are other ways to think about what is going on by recognizing that two quite separate matters overlap. One is whether the polls reliably predict elections in general, race aside. The other is whether voters have racist motives, either overt or covert, when they cast their ballots. The two questions are often linked: white voters may be dissembling in their support for the minority candidate or they may be hiding in the undecided column because the new racism is more subtle and covert than the old.

There is, however, no necessary reason to link unreliable polls and voting based on race. Race can affect votes without biasing poll results as long as people tell the truth when asked about their preferences. Conversely, poll results can be unreliable even if people do not care a whit about race; a campaign may make people's preferences volatile, voters may go with the front-runner until they begin to take an election more seriously, turnout may be uneven, and undecideds may vote in unpredictable ways because they are often the least knowledgeable or attentive members of the electorate. Of course, some of these conditions may interact with racial considerations: those who are undecided or who have gravitated toward the front-runner may ultimately base their choice on race.

Voters in districts in which a black candidate is running may also be more volatile because these campaigns draw so much attention from the news media. In the three cases discussed here, a win by the black candidate meant a historic first and a terrific news story. With the crescendo of coverage in the last week of the campaign, one would be surprised if voters stood pat.

Polls may also fail to predict the results in interracial campaigns because of racism—perhaps even old-fashioned racism. Bradley, Wilder, and Dinkins were black Democratic candidates pitted against white Republicans. This undoubtedly caused white Democratic voters to feel "cross-pressured" in much the same way Protestant Democrats were when John F. Kennedy, a Democrat and a Catholic, ran against Richard Nixon, a Protestant and a Republican, in 1960.[61]

In the 1982 Bradley election, for example, one study found no evidence that the Bradley effect resulted from whites hiding their support for the white candidate by responding "undecided" to polsters' questions.[62] Instead the inaccuracy may have resulted from cross-pressure, which may postpone the crystallization of candidate preference in the final days of the campaign and make predictions about winners less reliable. In the 1982 Bradley-Deukmejian race, the pressures of partisanship and race probably led white Democratic voters to remain undecided somewhat longer than if race had not been a factor. It probably also led white Democrats eventually to vote for Deukmejian. This dynamic also explains why undecided voters eventually vote for the white candidate; there is no need to invoke the new racism when the old may explain so much. And it helps explain what happened in the 1989 Chicago mayoralty election, where white Democrat Richard Daley ran against black independent Timothy Evans.[63] "This time, *black* voters faced a conflict between party and race. In this election, the late undecided vote was disproportionately black. And the final pre-election poll results proved to be an underestimation of the vote Evans ended up receiving."[64]

Cross-pressures occur in many campaigns, and they do not lend themselves to any easy rule of thumb. They can be reactions to factors other than race—gender, ethnicity, insider-outsider status—and they can work in different directions depending on the overall dynamics of the campaigns. More important, they do not lead to the conclusion that voters are dissembling when they respond to the pollster. The voters may be genuinely undecided about fundamental issues. The roots of this conflict may sometimes be racial, religious, or gender biases, but the conflict is undeniably real and important. It should be covered in the press in this way.[65]

Polls in interracial campaigns may be unreliable for the same reasons they are unreliable in many campaigns, and this illustrates the pitfalls facing those who would use surveys to make fine-grained predictions in any electoral campaign. Most of all, polling in interracial campaigns illustrates the need for better-specified theories about what affects people's responses to polls during campaigns.

THE DYNAMICS OF CAMPAIGNS. All preelection polls face the same problem. Because campaigns and the electorates they try to reach are inherently volatile, political opinion polls can provide a snapshot of the electorate at a given moment, but even a series of snapshots cannot substitute for a theory of campaign dynamics that can be used to interpret the pictures.

Even if journalists had been inclined to learn from political scientists, they could not have learned much about specifying a model of campaign dynamics until recently. The received wisdom among American political scientists was that campaigns do not matter.[66] But in the late 1980s academics began to take them seriously and to develop theories that might be useful to reporters.[67]

As research on campaign dynamics and polling liabilities grows, reporters have even less excuse for presenting survey data uncritically. A first step is to warn viewers and readers about the vagaries of polls. A second, however, is news coverage that reminds voters how fast changes have occurred in other campaigns, explores the causes of change, and emphasizes the issues at stake. This means more than simply reporting the margin of error or acknowledging the difficulty of measuring public opinion. It means attempting to explain what the entire electoral process is about and what part polls play in that process.

Theories, specified or not, drive the choices facing a pollster: who will be sampled, what questions will be asked, how the data will be interpreted. Thus, if theories of issue saliency are not prominently in mind, a poll might fail to differentiate between real attitudes and nonattitudes. Unless the pollster recognizes that political opinion expresses itself in terms of position, valence, and performance, a poll might equate people's attitudes only with their views on the substantive policy alternatives of a given issue. Similarly, preelection polling must be guided by theories of campaign dynamics that warn of such hazards as opinion volatility and hidden white votes.

Theory specification is essential not only for gathering data—designing appropriate samples and asking appropriate questions—but also for analyzing the data that result. As for analysis, media polls are regularly and badly underanalyzed because of the severe time and space limitations facing reporters and their perception that the limited tastes and capacities of the audience do not call for much analysis.

Recent advances in polling technology only reinforce these tendencies. High-speed computers merged with telephones enable pollsters to gather, analyze, and report opinions faster than ever before. As in other realms of computer technology, the usefulness of the end result is limited by the GIGO (garbage in, garbage out) principle. But computers are not theory-making machines, and no amount of technology can compensate for faulty original ideas. These initial flaws—the poorly specified hypotheses that underlie most media polls—are yet another reason poll reporting is so weak on analysis.

For example, during the 1990 Massachusetts gubernatorial campaign Democrat John Silber and Republican William Weld shared the ballot with several referenda including a proposal for immediate tax reduction.

Silber weighed in against the referendum, even though many moderate and conservative Democrats who were attracted to his conservative stands on social issues favored it. Weld favored the rollback, even though much of his support came from people who liked his liberal stands on social issues but opposed the referendum. But while the pages of the *Boston Globe* were filled with musings on how voters would juggle these apparent cross-pressures, and while the paper polled voters both on their gubernatorial preferences and on their attitudes toward the referendum, it did not use its poll data to analyze the ways voters viewed the two matters in conjunction. This underanalysis could have been avoided if even the most rudimentary theory of cross-pressures and campaign dynamics had guided the *Globe*'s polling. Unfortunately, this shortcoming is typical of news organizations throughout the country.

The antidote to specification error in any sort of poll is careful thinking and sound ideas. What academics call theories and hypotheses, journalists prefer to call arguments and hunches. Call it what you will. But preconceptions about political attitudes and behavior govern public opinion polling, whether the pollster is aware of it or not.

Conclusion

Using polls properly requires understanding not only sampling error and the many practical problems that accompany sampling, but also the difficulties of social measurement and the liabilities of implicit theoretical assumptions that can creep into the design and analysis of any poll. Sampling error, which receives virtually all the attention, is far less troublesome than measurement or specification error. Unfortunately, one cannot come to grips with these last two sources of error without a thorough grasp of the substance of a poll. There is no alternative. This places enormous burdens on researchers and pollsters alike, but it makes life even harder for journalists, who cannot be experts on every aspect of public policy and public opinion.

What, then, can be done? To begin with, journalists should think about the following steps toward improving their polls.

—Develop a better understanding of the nature and severity of falling response rates and establish minimum response-rate standards.

—Make fuller disclosure in news reports of sampling information, including response rates, particularly for local and regional surveys in news reports based on polls.

—Even more important, concentrate on the depth rather than the breadth of polling. That means investing more time and money in fewer surveys with larger samples, more callbacks, and more time for analysis and interpretation of results. The surveys that should be dropped from the polling repertoire first are the pernicious "quickie" polls.

—Cover fewer topics and ask more questions about each topic in each poll. The complexity of social measurement requires multiple questions to gauge any attitude. Expanding the number of questions per topic might permit some experimenting with different wordings in split samples. Here again, the rule of thumb should be depth before breadth.

—Give more attention to measuring the importance of topics for the people surveyed, including the respondents' levels of interest and knowledge and the stability of their responses over time.

—Carry out more penetrating analyses of polls, for example taking into account more than one variable at a time.

—Read at least some of the literature on public opinion and voting. Of course, this implies a corresponding assignment for the political scientists: make such material more accessible to nonexperts.

Polling is not like making instant coffee. The pitfalls awaiting those who hope to pick representative samples, accurately measure opinions, and wisely interpret the data are many and deep. And those pitfalls are especially deep for media polls, where the imperatives of good survey research clash with the pressures of journalism. The careful thought necessary to avoid the most serious methodological perils takes time. In polling, as on highways, speed kills.

Notes

1. Statisticians refer to two hypotheses. The null hypothesis is generally the assumption that no change has occurred in either the world or our understanding of it. The alternative hypothesis posits changes in the world or in our understanding of it. The common, everyday meaning of the word *hypothesis* is that it refers to a new or novel notion about the world. Our discussion uses *hypothesis* in this sense, which is equivalent to the statistician's *alternative hypothesis*.

2. V.O. Key, Jr., *Public Opinion and American Democracy* (Knopf, 1961), p. 8.

3. Carl Bernstein, "The Idiot Culture," *New Republic*, June 8, 1992, p. 24.

4. Henry E. Brady and Richard Johnston, "What's the Primary Message: Horse Race or Issue Journalism?" in Gary Orren and Nelson Polsby, eds., *Media and Momentum: The New Hampshire Primary and Nomination Politics* (Chatham House, 1988), pp. 127–86.

5. For an excellent introduction see Seymour Sudman, *Applied Sampling* (Academic Press, 1976).

6. Those with more than one home can only be in one at a time, so this is not a problem.

7. Owen T. Thornberry, Jr., and James T. Massey, "Trends in United States Telephone Coverage across Time and Subgroups," in Robert M. Groves and others, eds., *Telephone Survey Methodology* (John Wiley, 1988), pp. 25–49; and Robert M. Groves and Robert L. Kahn, *Surveys by Telephone: A National Comparison with Personal Interviews* (Academic Press, 1979), pp. 155–61 and table 6-1.

8. They are, from the most to the least intrusive (and from the most to the least accurate), the following. The interviewer asks for the gender and age of everyone in the household and then randomly selects a respondent from this list. Or the interviewer asks how many adults and how many men live in the household and then using alternative grids selects a respondent. Or the interviewer asks to speak with the person in the household who has had the most recent birthday. Or the interviewer asks for a man and interviews a woman only if no men are available. See Leslie Kish, "A Procedure for Objective Respondent Selection within the Household," *Journal of the American Statistical Association*, vol. 44 (September 1949), pp. 380–87; Verling C. Troldahl and Roy E. Carter, Jr., "Random Selection of Respondents within Households in Phone Surveys," *Journal of Marketing Research*, vol. 1 (May 1964), pp. 71–76; and Charles T. Salmon and John Spicer Nichols, "The Next-Birthday Method of Respondent Selection," *Public Opinion Quarterly*, vol. 47 (Spring 1983), pp. 270–76.

9. In the United States, the proportion of ineligible numbers is often as high as 80 percent (Groves and Kahn, *Surveys by Telephone*, p. 45). Of these, 6 percent might be businesses, 53 percent nonworking numbers indicated by a recording, 6 percent with no result from a dial, or a *"fastbusy,"* or a *"wrong connection,"* and 3 percent ring with no answer. Nonworking numbers with a recording are no problem, but businesses, fast busys, wrong connections, and ring-no-answers pose more difficult problems. Inevitably, even after many calls, some telephones are never answered or they are always busy. One study allowed as many as fifteen calls to determine the status of each number and ended with 4 percent of the numbers never answered or always busy. See note 10.

10. The principal investigators were Richard Johnston, Andre Blais, Henry E. Brady, and Jean Crete. The study was conducted by the Institute for Social Research, York University, Ontario.

11. Michael W. Traugott, "The Importance of Persistence in Respondent Selection for Pre-election Surveys," *Public Opinion Quarterly*, vol. 51 (Spring 1987), pp. 48–57.

12. John Brehm, "Opinion Surveys and Political Representation," Ph.D. dissertation, University of Michigan, 1990, p. 20.

13. Randall Rothenberg, "Surveys Proliferate, but Answers Dwindle," *New York Times*, October 5, 1990, pp. A1, D4; and Tom Piazza, "Overcoming the Answering Machine Barrier," working paper, Survey Research Center, University of California, Berkeley, 1992.

14. Brehm, "Opinion Surveys and Political Representation," pp. 77, 87. Similar findings emerged from the Canadian study discussed earlier. Probably the most important event of the 1988 Canadian campaign was a debate on October 25 in which John Turner, head of the Liberal party, accused Tory Prime Minister Brian Mulroney of selling out Canada in agreeing to free trade with the United States. Turner's performance ignited the Liberal party and changed the dynamics of the entire campaign. After the debate, 59 percent of those interviewed on the first call to a household said they saw the debate; 49 percent of those who required three or more calls saw it. These results suggest that simple reweighting may not be the best way to correct surveys. Unfortunately, better methods, other than reducing nonresponse through more callbacks, require considerable technical sophistication and substantial information about the nonrespondents. See Christopher H. Achen, *The Statistical Analysis of Quasi-Experiments* (University of California Press, 1986); James J. Heckman, "The Common Structure of Statistical Models of Truncation, Sample Selection, and Limited Dependent Variables and a Simple Estimator for Such Models," *Annals of Economic and Social Measurement*, vol. 5 (1976), pp. 475–92; Heckman, "Sample Selection

Bias as a Specification Error," *Econometrica*, vol. 47 (January 1979), pp. 153–61; and Brehm, "Opinion Surveys and Political Representation."

15. See Rothenberg, "Surveys Proliferate"; and Walker Research, *Industry Image Study*, 8th ed. (Indianapolis, 1988). For nonresponse rates see Charlotte G. Steeth, "Trends in Nonresponse Rates, 1952–1979," *Public Opinion Quarterly*, vol. 45 (Spring 1981), pp. 40–57; and Robert M. Groves and Lars E. Lyberg, "An Overview of Nonresponse Issues in Telephone Surveys," in Groves and others, eds., *Telephone Survey Methodology*, pp. 203–06.

16. Response rates for instant polls are estimated from limited data provided by one of the national media polling organizations.

17. Also needing further study is whether announcing at the beginning of an interview that the poll is sponsored by a particular news organization reduces cooperation rates if that organization is identified with a particular editorial point of view. One study found evidence of this in some *Washington Post* polls. See Stanley Presser, Johnny Blair, and Timothy Triplett, "Survey Sponsorship, Cooperation Rates, and Response Effects: A Research Note," Survey Research Center, University of Maryland, February 1991.

18. Brehm, "Opinion Surveys and Political Representation."

19. *Public Perspective*, vol. 3 (March–April 1992), included four articles on this CBS program: "Program Excerpts," pp. 18–19; "The CBS News Call-In: 'Slipups in the Broadcast'— Interview with Kathleen Frankovic," pp. 19–21; "The CBS News Call-In: 'First and Foremost . . . Bad Information'—Interview with Warren Mitofsky," pp. 22–23; and Albert H. Cantril, "The CBS News Call-In: A Setback for All Public Polls," pp. 23–24. The CBS call-in program reminds one of the more embarrassing moments in the history of polling. In 1936 *Literary Digest* distributed 10 million mock presidential ballots to a sample of Americans drawn from telephone directories and automobile registries. The responses from this biased sample of upper-status, pro-Republican adults predicted that Alf Landon would win in a landslide. Franklin Roosevelt actually trounced Landon 61 percent to 37 percent.

20. Beginning in 1990 ABC, CBS, and NBC, which had been conducting exit polls independently, pooled their resources along with CNN to form a consortium, Voter Research & Surveys. Other news organizations, including the *New York Times*, the *Washington Post*, *USA Today*, and Knight-Ridder, have subscribed to this service. Kathleen Francovic in this book discusses this significant change in exit poll administration.

21. Mark R. Levy, "The Methodology and Performance of Election Day Polls," *Public Opinion Quarterly*, vol. 47 (Spring 1983), p. 59.

22. Warren J. Mitofsky, "What Went Wrong with Exit Polling in New Hampshire?" *Public Perspective*, vol. 3 (March–April 1992), p. 17.

23. Thomas Whippman, ed., *The Washington Post Deskbook on Style* (McGraw-Hill, 1989), p. 167.

24. "Reporting on Polls or Surveys," CBS News, April 17, 1978.

25. In most cases we required that the description of the population include the type of person (registered voters, adults, members of Congress) and the geographic area involved (Cook County, United States, rural Mexican communities).

26. The difficulties of social measurement are described in Otis Dudley Duncan, *Notes on Social Measurement: Historical and Critical* (Russell Sage, 1984).

27. The following discussion is based on Gary Orren, "Presidential Popularity Ratings: Another View," *Public Opinion*, vol. 1 (May–June, 1978), p. 35.

28. The differences also are due in part to the contrasting question formats: the Harris question used a one-sided format; the *New York Times*/CBS News question used a two-sided format, as discussed below.

29. Milton J. Rosenberg, Sidney Verba, and Philip E. Converse, *Vietnam and the Silent Majority: The Dove's Guide* (Harper and Row, 1970), pp. 23–30.

30. For example, Howard Schuman and Stanley Presser, *Questions and Answers in*

Attitude Surveys: Experiments on Question Form, Wording, and Context (Academic Press, 1981); and Seymour Sudman and Norman M Bradburn, *Asking Questions: A Practical Guide to Questionnaire Design* (Jossey-Bass, 1989). *Public Opinion Quarterly* has published many studies on the consequences of alternative wording, format, and question ordering.

31. Schuman and Presser, *Questions and Answers in Attitude Surveys*, p. 281.

32. For a discussion of these and other common mistakes see Sudman and Bradburn, *Asking Questions*.

33. Philip E. Converse, "The Nature of Belief Systems in Mass Publics," in David Apter, ed., *Ideology and Discontent* (Free Press, 1964), pp. 206–61.

34. Lloyd A. Free and Hadley Cantril, *The Political Beliefs of Americans: A Study of Public Opinion* (Rutgers University Press, 1967), chap. 3.

35. Christopher H. Achen, "Mass Political Attitudes and the Survey Response," *American Political Science Review*, vol. 69 (December 1975), pp. 1218–31.

36. Donald R. Kinder and David O. Sears, "Public Opinion and Political Action," in Gardner Lindzey and Elliot Aronson, eds., *The Handbook of Social Psychology*, vol. 2, 3d ed. (Random House, 1984), p. 670.

37. Larry M. Bartels, *Presidential Primaries and the Dynamics of Public Choice* (Princeton University Press, 1988), pp. 65–83; and Brady and Johnston, "What's the Primary Message?"

38. National Election Studies Surveys, Inter University Consortium for Political and Social Research.

39. Brady and Johnston, "What's the Primary Message?"

40. See Elizabeth Kolbert, "From Florida, A Cautionary Lesson on Perception," *New York Times*, March 12, 1992, p. A19. The danger of basing preelection news reports on stale data was demonstrated dramatically as early as 1948 when George Gallup stopped polling on October 25, assuming that Thomas Dewey's lead over Harry Truman was insurmountable.

41. Glenn Dempsey, Ph.D. research, University of Chicago, 1991.

42. Thomas Hardy, "Simon Leading Martin, but It's Not Set in Stone," *Chicago Tribune*, December 25, 1989, p. 1.

43. Kathleen A. Frankovic, "Reading Between the Polls," *New York Times*, June 27, 1992, p. 23.

44. See Roger Tourangeau and Kenneth A. Rasinski, "Cognitive Processes Underlying Context Effects and Attitude Measurement," *Psychological Bulletin*, vol. 103, no. 3 (1988), pp. 299–314.

45. Converse, "Nature of Belief Systems in Mass Publics," pp. 206–61.

46. Polls should also emphasize questions measuring saliency because, even though the direction of opinion changes glacially for most issues, saliency can and does change rapidly.

47. Paul F. Lazarsfeld, Bernard Berelson, and Hazel Gaudet, *The People's Choice: How the Voter Makes Up His Mind in a Presidential Campaign* (Columbia University Press, 1944); and Bernard Berelson, Paul F. Lazarsfeld, and William N. McPhee, *Voting: A Study of Opinion Formation in a Presidential Campaign* (University of Chicago Press, 1954).

48. Angus Campbell and others, *The American Voter* (John Wiley, 1960).

49. V.O. Key, Jr., *The Responsible Electorate: Rationality in Presidential Voting, 1936–1960* (Harvard University Press, 1966); David E. Repass, "Issue Salience and Party Choice," *American Political Science Review*, vol. 65 (June 1971), pp. 389–400; Richard W. Boyd, "Popular Control of Public Policy: A Normal Vote Analysis of the 1968 Election," *American Political Science Review*, vol. 66 (June 1972), pp. 429–49; John Kessel, "Comment: The Issues in Issue Voting," *American Political Science Review*, vol. 66 (June 1972), pp. 459–65; Norman Nie, Sidney Verba, and John Petrocik, *The Changing American Voter* (Harvard University Press, 1976); and Morris P. Fiorina, *Retrospective Voting in American National Elections* (Yale University Press, 1981).

50. Benajamin I. Page and Richard A. Brody, "Policy Voting and the Electoral Process: The Vietnam Issue," *American Political Science Review*, vol. 66 (September 1972), pp. 979–95.

51. Indeed, among those who cast votes in the 1968 New Hampshire Democratic presidential primary for Senator Eugene McCarthy, an outspoken dovish critic of the Johnson administration, the number of hawks outnumbered the number of doves three to two. This is puzzling only if it is assumed that McCarthy voters were motivated by the war as a position issue. In fact, both hawks and doves were rejecting Lyndon Johnson's handling of the war by voting for his opponent. See Philip E. Converse and others, "Continuity and Change in American Politics: Parties and Issues in the 1968 Election," *American Political Science Review*, vol. 63 (December 1969), pp. 1083–1105.

52. The first differentiation of position and valence issues appeared in David Butler and Donald Stokes, *Political Change in Britain* (St. Martin's Press, 1971), p. 177: "Many issues present alternative policies or conditions whose value is a matter of disagreement in the country . . . but other issues . . . involve a virtual consensus in the electorate, and indeed among the parties as well, on the values entailed by different alternatives. . . . There is no body of opinion in the country that favors economic distress, and thereby cancels some of the votes of those who want better times; the whole weight of opinion lies on the side of prosperity and growth. Issues of this sort do not find the parties positioning themselves to appeal to those who favor alternative policies or goals. Rather the parties attempt to associate themselves in the public's mind with conditions, such as good times, which are universally favored, and to dissociate themselves from conditions, such as economic distress, which are universally deplored. Such a distinction between *position* issues, on which the parties may appeal to rival bodies of opinion, and *valence* issues, on which there is essentially one body of opinion on values or goals, is too often neglected in political commentary. But the parties themselves are well aware of the potential of such valence issues as peace and economic prosperity and national prestige."

53. Thomas Piazza, Paul Sniderman, and Philip Tetlock, "Analysis of the Dynamics of Political Reasoning: A General Purpose Computer Assisted Methodology," in James A. Stimson, ed., *Political Analysis: An Annual Publication of the Methodology Section of the American Political Science Association*, vol. 1 (University of Michigan Press, 1989).

54. Donald R. Kinder, "The Continuing American Dilemma: White Resistance to Racial Change 40 Years after Myrdal," *Journal of Social Issues*, vol. 42, no. 2 (1986), pp. 151–71.

55. Paul M. Sniderman and Philip E. Tetlock, "Reflections on American Racism," *Journal of Social Issues*, vol. 42, no. 2 (1986), pp. 173–87; and Kinder, "Continuing American Dilemma."

56. These numbers are based on data in Thomas F. Pettigrew and Denise A. Alston, *Tom Bradley's Campaigns for Governor: The Dilemma of Race and Political Strategies*, (Washington: Joint Center for Political Studies, 1988), table 1 and p. 12.

57. Data compiled from Owen Shapiro, "The Bradley Effect in Three Elections: California (1982), Virginia (1989), New York City (1989)," M.A. thesis, University of Chicago, 1990, p. 42. Three polls were completed by the *Washington Post* and two by Mason-Dixon Opinion Research. We draw heavily upon this study in this section.

58. Shapiro, "Bradley Effect," p. 51. The average is based on eight polls completed between mid-October and early November. A *Newsday* poll and a *New York Observer* poll have been omitted because very little information was available on them. There were three *Daily News*/WABC polls, two other *Newsday* polls, two other *New York Observer* polls, and one Teamster poll.

59. The one possible exception is the Mason Dixon poll of November 1, 1989, which showed 48 percent for Wilder, 44 percent for Coleman, and 8 percent undecided. Using

the rule would have made Coleman the winner at 52 percent to 48 percent for Wilder. Pettigrew and Alston, "Tom Bradley's Campaign for Governor."

60. Pettigrew and Alston "Tom Bradley's Campaign for Governor," p. 83, refer to "modern racism" or the "new racism," which amounts to "subtle, somewhat ambiguous racial code words and campaign slogans such as Deukmejian's 'He can represent all of the state's people.'" The definition is closely related to symbolic racism in its emphasis on the subtlety, but it is not as closely tied to ideas of American individualism as symbolic racism, in which "whites' opposition to racial change reflects their endorsement of racist sentiments and traditional American values, particularly individualism." Kinder, "Continuing American Dilemma," p. 151.

61. The idea of cross-pressures was first advanced in Berelson, Lazarsfeld, and McPhee, *Voting*.

62. Shapiro, "Bradley Effect," pp. 55–56.

63. Evans was a Democrat, but he decided to oppose Richard Daley in the general election by forming the Harold Washington party, named after the recently deceased black mayor of Chicago.

64. Larry Hugick in a paper delivered at the 1989 meeting of the New York chapter of the American Association for Public Opinion Research, quoted in Richard Morin, "Another Theory about the Error of Their Ways," *Washington Post National Weekly Edition*, December 11–17, 1989, p. 37.

65. There may also be some dissembling by voters, but we suspect that it is much less important than cross-pressures.

66. The classic Columbia University studies of campaigns (Lazarsfeld, Berelson, and Gaudet, *The People's Choice*; Berelson, Lazarsfeld, and McPhee, *Voting*) used repeated interviews of voters to look for campaign effects but concluded that campaigns do not matter that much. The next major wave of election studies completed at the University of Michigan (Campbell and others, *American Voter*) were not designed to find campaign effects because they relied on interviews conducted just before and after elections. One book on predicting election outcomes, Steven J. Rosenstone, *Forecasting Presidential Elections* (Yale University Press, 1983), even argued that all that really matters in an election is the state of the economy and the liberalism or conservatism of the candidates. Campaign events are basically irrelevant. A few dissents have appeared in the thirty years since the Columbia studies— for example, Thomas E. Patterson, *The Mass Media Election: How Americans Choose Their President* (Praeger, 1980)—but American political scientists have mostly concluded that campaigns are not very important.

67. In 1980, 1984, and 1988 the National Election studies started to use designs that tracked changes during campaigns, and research started to reflect a new attitude toward campaigns. The first breakthrough came with the study of primaries (see Brady and Johnston, "What's the Primary Message?"; and Bartels, *Presidential Primaries*, both from the late 1980s). These showed that media coverage and expectations about candidates were especially important during the nomination process. More recently, studies of general elections have used other data: media and commercial polls in the United States and a "rolling cross-section" in Canada. See Samuel Popkin, *The Reasoning Voter: Communication and Persuasion in Presidential Campaigns* (University of Chicago Press, 1991); and Richard Johnston and others, *Letting the People Decide* (Montreal: McGill-Queens Press, forthcoming).

In these books, political scientists have begun to take campaigns seriously and propose theories in which political rhetoric, debates, serendipitous events, strategic voting, the mobilization and nonmobilization of voters, advertising, and the mass media play a dynamic role. For example, *Letting the People Decide* analyzes the ups and downs of a three-party race in Canada. It shows how the governing Conservative party called an election to show support for free trade; how the issue almost backfired on them after a vigorous attack by the leader of the opposition Liberal party in a televised debate halfway through the campaign; how the third party, the New Democrats, added to the unpredictability of the campaign; and how news media coverage and advertising eventually turned the tide back toward the Conservatives. The study is one of startling reverses, some of which took place within a few days. The lesson for poll watchers is that substantial changes can occur quickly and that they are based on events in the campaigns, not just on long-term forces that already existed.

Chapter 5

Variability without Fault: Why Even Well-Designed Polls Can Disagree

MICHAEL R. KAGAY

M OST OF the major national polls today are reasonably well designed and competently conducted, with pollsters having absorbed many of the lessons discussed in the previous chapter. Yet, as any close observer can attest, these polls disagree fairly frequently for reasons involving no obvious methodological error, sin, or negligence. And even if any remaining methodological shortcomings were successfully rooted out, polls would continue to yield results that are sometimes discrepant and occasionally contradictory. Such no-fault variability essentially occurs because of the pluralism in the polling profession.

From the mid-1930s, when modern public opinion polling was established by George Gallup, Elmo Roper, and Archibald Crossley, until the mid-1970s, only two or three organizations at any given time conducted national polls and made their results publicly available. Poll findings came to the attention of the public infrequently, and even if two organizations

I wish to thank colleagues at all the organizations whose poll results are cited in this chapter for designing, conducting, and making publicly available an extraordinary range of instructive studies of public opinion in America. I also thank Adam Clymer, who oversaw polling at the *New York Times* from 1983 to early 1990; he collaborated in the early planning of this chapter, and I regret that because of his new duties at the *Times* he was unable to help write it. I am also indebted to Marjorie Connelly, Janet Elder, and Deborah Hofmann of the New Surveys Department at the *Times*, who originally computed, checked, and scrupulously organized the numerical material drawn from the *New York Times*/CBS News polls. Additional thanks to the *Times*'s partners in polling at CBS News: Warren Mitofsky, Martin Plissner, and especially Kathleen Frankovic. Finally, I am grateful for especially insightful and generous suggestions from Richard Morin, polling director at the *Washington Post*.

released findings within days or weeks of one another, the polls often covered different topics. Therefore variations or discrepancies in results did not often arise except just before presidential elections when each poll was, quite naturally, trying to measure the same thing. In the past decade, however, with as many as ten organizations conducting national polls and releasing the results to the public, chances are fairly high that in any given month or even week polls will treat the same topic, often in different ways and sometimes with discrepant findings.

The likelihood of multiple polls on the same topic has increased not just because of the proliferation of polls but also because of who the new pollsters are. Many of the polling agencies that have begun operating since the mid-1970s are sponsored by news organizations. They are not polling for the ages nor to test academic theories; they are polling for news and are likely to focus on topics that are timely and thus also of interest to other news organizations that same week or month. But the same competitive instincts that encourage these organizations to investigate similar topics also prompt them to approach the topics from fresh and distinctive angles. Indeed, if the results of a poll are not original in some way, they will not qualify as news. Thus once a news organization establishes its own poll, it has an incentive to seek its own approach to topics, develop its own wording of questions, and discover its own nuances in analyzing, interpreting, and presenting the results—within, of course, the boundaries of methods accepted by the polling profession. Variability necessarily follows.

When the results of several polls on the same subject appear contradictory, which—if any—is to be believed? Only on election day is there a hard reality check against which to measure them. When polls on domestic policy or foreign policy issues seem to disagree, the potential for creating confusion is significant. Members of the public might be forgiven for shrugging, taking cynical attitudes, and questioning the legitimacy of all opinion polls.

But for the close observer, the recent proliferation of polls is a boon. Ironically, proliferation helps provide its own check, allowing the self-correcting tendencies of the polling profession to assert themselves more quickly than would otherwise be the case. Thus, proliferation entails the virtues as well as the difficulties associated with pluralism.

This chapter examines instances of variability among recent American public opinion polls on three quite different topics: the standing of candidates during presidential election years, the war in the Persian Gulf, and the controversy over abortion. Each topic encompasses factors that can cause even well-designed polls to arrive at discrepant findings. The discussion alerts observers on what to look for—and what to watch out for—in judging poll results.

Presidential Election Polls

Presidential election polls make interesting subjects because polling organizations are presumably trying their best to estimate the same thing, and for each, election day looms as a day of reckoning. Yet even so, major election polls that are equally well conducted can give discrepant results.

Timing: The Postconvention Bounce

Although polls during the last week of an election campaign are conducted within days of one another, earlier in the year organizations may conduct them at quite different times, between which important events can occur that sometimes change the balance of public opinion. For example, in the summer before, during, and just after the Democratic and Republican nominating conventions, polls conducted at different times can register dramatically different results. Typically, candidates get a boost from receiving their party's official anointment and bask in attention and acclaim. But because several weeks separate the convention dates of the two parties, the nominee of the first convention soars in public approval while the other party's candidate unavoidably languishes before gaining his own postconvention boost. Polls containing trial heats of candidates' strength during this time can give a temporary and unrealistic picture of their underlying standings.

The Gallup Organization documented this effect vividly in polls conducted during 1988 before and after each party's nominating convention. Michael Dukakis rocketed out of the Democratic convention to take a 17-percentage-point lead over George Bush, but the lead quickly shrank and after the Republican convention became a deficit (table 5-1). Most of the public movement, first toward Dukakis and then away, came from independents, swayed by images and messages surrounding each convention.

Much journalistic ink is wasted at this time of the campaign year in attempts to explain how one candidate's ineptness has frittered away certain victory while the other candidate's brilliant strategy has overcome

Table 5-1. *Presidential Candidate Standings before and after Democratic and Republican Party Conventions, 1988*
Percent

| Period | Party affiliation | Voter preference | | | Sample size (registered voters) |
		Bush	Dukakis	Other, undecided	
Before Democratic	Republicans	85	8	7	317
Convention	Independents	39	42	19	357
(July 8–10)	Democrats	5	85	10	327
	Total	41	47	12	1,001
After Democratic	Republicans	76	16	8	319
Convention	Independents	32	53	15	315
(July 22–24)	Democrats	8	87	5	367
	Total	37	54	9	1,001
Before Republican	Republicans	76	13	11	336
Convention	Independents	43	44	13	368
(August 5–7)	Democrats	6	92	2	300
	Total	42	49	9	1,004
After Republican	Republicans	90	6	n.a.	n.a.
Convention	Independents	47	38	n.a.	n.a.
(August 19–21)	Democrats	8	87	n.a.	n.a.
	Total	48	44	8	1,000
After Labor Day	Republicans	89	7	4	328
(September 9–11)	Independents	48	35	17	367
	Democrats	10	82	8	308
	Total	49	41	10	1,003

Source: *Gallup Report*, no. 275 (August 1988), pp. 14–15; no. 276 (September 1988), p. 3; no. 277 (October 1988), p. 10; and Gallup Poll release, August 24, 1988.
n.a. Not available.

a fatal deficit. Responsible reporting of poll results becomes particularly important at this stage so that a temporary or artificial advantage will not be portrayed as lasting and the subsequent collapse of that advantage will not provoke consternation or unwarranted dismay. Some journalists automatically discount the results of polls conducted between conventions, sometimes referring to the strength of the leading candidate as a postconvention "bounce" that will probably prove short-lived, and sometimes recalling other election years when similarly temporary advantages vanished. In reporting its 1988 results, for example, Gallup referred prominently to the 1984 campaign, when Walter Mondale's nomination allowed him to rival Ronald Reagan's strength in the polls for a few weeks before he fell behind again.[1]

Uncrystallized Opinions Can Be Unstable

A problem related to timing is whether opinion has sufficiently crystallized when a poll is conducted. As a new issue develops or a new candidacy gathers steam, people learn more about it, become more familiar with its implications, and gradually firm up their views. But at early stages, opinions may be ill-formed and unstable, and people's knowledge of issues and candidates may be so thin that almost any new information can overwhelm what they know. For example, in July 1988 a higher percentage of registered voters had a favorable opinion of Michael Dukakis than of George Bush. But even though Dukakis had won numerous primaries and held a strong lead in convention delegates, even more voters said they were "undecided" or had "not heard enough" about him (table 5-2). This signaled a clear opportunity for the Bush campaign to provide voters with new information about Dukakis that would help define him in ways advantageous to Republicans. By late summer, as people learned more about Dukakis, many came not to like what they saw or heard, and public opinion turned against him.

Effects of Question Placement and Context

Respondents generally try to answer poll questions they think they are being asked, and they respond within the context in which the questions are asked. Thus pollsters using differently worded questions can sometimes get discrepant results even when the topics seem the same. And questions with the same wording can yield divergent results if pollsters ask them in different contexts by placing them at noncomparable locations in their questionnaires.

Many pollsters traditionally ask respondents whom they would vote for near the beginning of their questionnaire, often after initial questions about likelihood of voting or familiarity with names of the major candidates. Their objective is to avoid contaminating voter preference with other questions that explore selected issues or candidate traits, questions that are likely to change from poll to poll as the campaign develops. For example, the Republican party is often associated with advocating a strong military defense, and the Democratic party with helping or caring about people in need. If one questionnaire asks whom the respondent intends to vote for after a series of questions stressing poverty, homelessness, and health care while another questionnaire initially poses questions stressing

Table 5-2. *Voter Opinion of Michael Dukakis and George Bush, October 1987–November 1988*
Percent

Date of poll	Dukakis				Bush				Sample size[a]
	Favorable	Not favorable	Undecided	Not heard enough	Favorable	Not favorable	Undecided	Not heard enough	
1987									
October 18–22	15	10	16	59	45	25	26	4	1,058
November 20–24	13	10	20	57	38	27	29	6	1,227
1988									
January 30–31	n.a.	n.a.	n.a.	n.a.	31	28	27	12	912
March 19–22	29	17	25	29	34	35	23	8	1,271
May 9–12	38	14	26	21	33	35	21	10	1,056
July 5–8	28	21	33	17	26	31	26	15	947
July 31–August 3	38	19	31	10	27	33	29	9	941
August 19–21	32	25	29	13	39	25	27	8	1,282
September 8–11	28	31	31	9	39	27	27	6	1,159
September 21–23	29	31	28	10	37	30	26	5	883
October 1–3	32	33	28	7	38	30	26	5	1,136
October 8–10	29	38	26	6	41	31	22	3	1,115
October 21–24	31	42	23	4	45	30	21	2	1,391
November 2–4	32	40	25	3	44	34	19	2	1,542

Sources: "*New York Times*/CBS News Poll Pre-election Poll," November 2–4, 1988; "CBS News/*New York Times* October Survey," October 1987; "CBS News/*New York Times* National Survey," November 1987; and "*New York Times* Survey on Dan Rather/George Bush Interview," January 1988. Refusals are not shown.
n.a. Not available (question not asked).
a. Registered voters.

military defense issues, the Democratic candidate might do better in the first and the Republican in the second.

But some other pollsters deliberately introduce contamination into their questionnaires. By asking questions about certain issues or traits of the candidates before asking the respondent his or her choice, they seek to simulate learning that they presume voters will undergo during the campaign. This technique can be particularly useful to a candidate's private pollster in market testing campaign themes. But using the technique can result in findings different from those reported by pollsters who simply measure voter preferences as they stand at the moment.

Louis Harris and Associates demonstrated during the 1984 presidential campaign just how much difference a simple shift in question placement can make. In a July poll, near the beginning of the questionnaire and before other topics had been raised, the Harris survey asked a randomly selected half of its respondents to choose between Reagan and Mondale. The remaining respondents were asked to choose later in the questionnaire, after a dozen questions had explored criticisms, negative attributes, and issue liabilities of each candidate. When the choice between candidates was made near the beginning of the interview, Reagan led Mondale 52 percent to 42 percent. When the choice was made later in the interview, after the analysis of each candidate's negatives, Reagan led only 50 percent to 47 percent.[2] Some of the difference, of course, could have been due to sampling error or other random effects, but the size and direction of the shift were sufficient to convince several Harris staff members of the importance of question placement.

Of course, which set of figures more accurately predicts the outcome of the election depends on the prescience of the pollsters in anticipating what voters will or will not learn by the end of the campaign. Deliberately contaminating a poll can be risky. News reports of poll results seldom say anything about the placement or context of particular questions, so that even close observers may not realize when they have encountered a placement effect. But most national polling organizations will provide copies of their questionnaires upon request and most now donate their data sets and documentation to survey archives, so peculiarities of question placement can eventually come to light.

Differences in Who Is Polled

Not all polls are intended to be projectable to the same population, and samples intentionally defined in different ways can generate different results. For instance, some polls are designed to represent all adults. Others interview only registered voters (about 70 percent of all adults). Still others seek to represent the most likely voters or to simulate a probable electorate. Because only 50 to 55 percent of the voting age population has cast ballots in recent presidential elections, a pollster who seeks to identify actual voters must disregard or discount the opinions of one of every two people encountered. Although some pollsters employ elaborate methods of screening voters during interviews or of weighting them differently afterward, there is no single generally accepted method for identifying those likely to vote. Thus even when two pollsters attempt the same task, they usually go about it in different ways.

Results of polls, therefore, may differ because by design they represent different populations. During 1988 the more tightly that pollsters squeezed their samples to identify those who might actually vote, the more pro-Republican the results became. Thus George Bush tended to do better in polls of likely voters than in polls of all registered voters, and he tended to do better in polls of all registered voters than in polls of the total adult population.[3]

Adding to the potential confusion, different polling organizations introduce their preferred methods at different stages of the election year. Some begin the year using all registered voters and then switch to a tighter screening or weighting procedure in the summer as the party nominees become clear. Others wait until after Labor Day when the fall campaign traditionally begins. Still others wait until the weeks just before the election on the grounds that opinion has by then solidified and merits the use of more precise methods. A few stick with the initial method for the entire year.[4]

Thus at any given moment, chances are that different organizations are basing their results on differently defined samples. A responsible news report will always tell the audience how a poll's sample was defined.

Differences in Pursuing Hard-to-Reach Respondents

Polls differ in the resources they devote to pursuing elusive or reluctant respondents. Because such respondents may have characteristics different from those of people who are easier to interview, polls with different pursuit procedures may arrive at somewhat different findings.[5]

Polls differ, for instance, in how many telephone calls they will make to find someone at home or to reach a designated respondent in the household. They also differ in the extent of their efforts to call back respondents who initially refuse the survey to try to persuade them to be interviewed.

Most polling organizations have a basic pursuit strategy for all or most of their election polls. Differences in their methods may be known to some polling experts, but it is very difficult for the more casual observer to learn about or take into account the effects of such differences.

Differences in Analysis and Reporting

Polling organizations sometimes employ different strategies of analyzing and reporting results. Some polls routinely press respondents who initially say they are undecided to declare which candidate they lean toward. The leaners can then be allocated to the appropriate candidate's supporters during analysis. Other polls may not identify leaners, or may identify them but as a matter of policy refrain from allocating them. For those voters who say they are undecided and do not know which way they lean, a few pollsters will bring elaborate methods to bear to allocate them according to which candidate's followers they most resemble in personal characteristics and attitudes toward issues. These differences in procedure can result in polls that give somewhat different impressions of which candidate is leading and by how much.

Even news organizations that work in partnership may follow different policies. In the final preelection results of the *New York Times*/CBS News poll in 1988, self-declared leaners were allocated in reports by CBS News but as a matter of policy were not allocated in reports by the *New York Times*.[6]

Sampling Error

Sampling error can cause results of different polls to diverge from one another, and the potential for it is always present no matter how well a survey is conducted. But it is one of the least of our concerns because the margin of error is calculable and its range can be stipulated in reporting results. Besides, in well-designed national surveys of standard size (for example, polls using random digit dialing methods with more than 1,000 interviews) the margin of sampling error is fairly small, typically 3 percentage points in either direction (at the 95 percent confidence level). The effects of many other factors can be considerably larger, more difficult to calculate, and often much harder to recognize.

The Day of Reckoning

The accuracy of preelection polls is usually gauged by comparing the final polls with the outcome of the vote.[7] When assessed in that way, the final national polls in the 1984 and 1988 presidential elections as a group were fairly accurate (figure 5-1). As a group they straddled or bracketed the actual election outcome: some polls were slightly high, some slightly low, but most were within the margin of sampling error. Those patterns were as they should have been if the polling methods were adequate to their task. Because all pollsters were trying to estimate the same population characteristic using probability samples, their estimates, according to probability theory, ought to have clustered fairly closely around the true population value. In each year, of course, some polls proved closer to the actual vote than others, and even as a group the polls seemed to bunch a little more tightly around the true result in 1988 than they did in 1984. But in either year if the results of the final polls had simply been averaged, the figure would have been very close to the actual results.

In the 1980 presidential election, however, all the polls underestimated the size of Ronald Reagan's victory. When all the polls are off to one side of the outcome, it is a sure sign of systematic difficulty. Initially, some observers alleged a hidden strength of Reagan as a candidate that may have existed all along but failed to register in polls conducted by the methods that were then standard. However, most pollsters concluded that a shift toward Reagan occurred after the polls had been completed or a disproportionate number of Carter supporters stayed home on election day, or perhaps both.[8]

In both 1984 and 1988 observers should have felt better served by the polls. One contributing reason was that after the inaccuracy in 1980 most pollsters found ways to poll as near to election day as possible to better detect any late shifts in voters' choices and intention of voting.

Conclusion

The range of acceptable polling methods remains wide enough to permit many legitimate variations in techniques and, consequently, in results.[9] This is so even though political pollsters have every incentive to see that their results are as close as possible to the outcome on election day. The proliferation of national polls makes the identification of quirky results, flukes, and blips much easier and quicker than formerly. But the sophisticated observer needs to be aware of the subtle differences between

Figure 5-1. *Leading Presidential Candidates' Margins in Final Preelection Polls, by Organization, 1980, 1984, 1988*

Percentage points

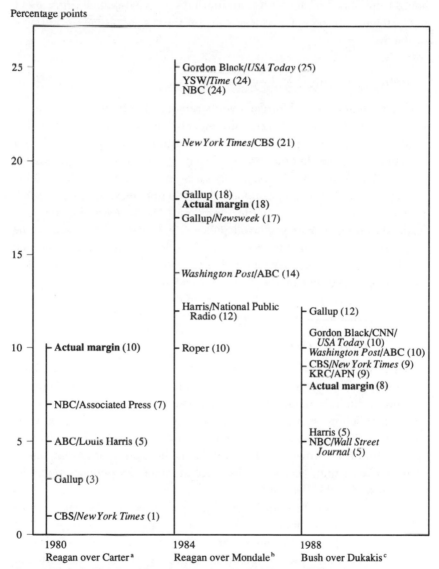

Source: *Public Opinion* vol. 3 (December–January 1981), p. 19; vol. 7 (October–November 1984), p. 40; and vol. 11 (November–December 1988), p. 39; and Bureau of the Census, *Statistical Abstract of the United States 1990* (Department of Commerce, 1990) p. 244
In some of the joint broadcast-print ventures, partners report figures in slightly different ways.
a. Average margin 4 percentage points for Reagan.
b. Average margin 18 percentage points for Reagan.
c. Average margin 9 percentage points for Bush.

equally well conducted polls that can still lead to discrepancies in results. Moreover, one might hope to learn from polls things other than who is ahead—the mood of the electorate, perhaps, or what people think about national and international issues. Polls on these matters have additional problems.

Polls on Foreign Policy

Many Americans find foreign events remote from their lives and often have at their disposal little accurate information about them. Although a small segment of the population may constitute an attentive public for foreign policy issues in quiet times, during international crises this public can swell enormously. At such times the critical question for polling usually becomes, how much support does the public extend to its leaders in dealing with the crisis, and for how long? Occasionally the country's leadership divides over preferred policies, with each faction promoting its policy and appealing for citizens to take sides. In such a situation, poll results become particularly vulnerable to the kinds of information, cues, or symbols contained in the questions and to the nature of the policy options offered to respondents. Even small differences can stimulate a large difference in public responses.

Policy Options Matter

The policy options offered for respondents to choose among can have a major impact on the answers given to a poll. And differing sets of options offered by different polling organizations can give an impression of seeming contradictions in the public's preferences. In December 1990 and January 1991, after the United Nations had authorized all necessary means to oust Iraq from Kuwait, different polls in the United States presented sharply contrasting pictures of the level of American public support for going to war in the Persian Gulf.

Polls that posed the alternatives as "use force or not" consistently registered majority support for war. For example, a *Washington Post/* ABC News poll taken November 30 to December 2 asked, "If Iraq does not withdraw from Kuwait, should the United States go to war with Iraq to force it out of Kuwait at some point after January 15, or not?" Some 63 percent responded yes to war, 32 percent responded no, and 5 percent expressed no opinion.[10] A *Wall Street Journal/*NBC News poll conducted December 8 to December 11 asked a slightly different question that offered essentially the same policy options: "Would you favor or oppose the U.S. going to war against Iraq if Iraq does not withdraw its troops from Kuwait by the United Nations' deadline of January 15?" The *Journal* reported that 54 percent of respondents favored war, 34 percent were opposed, and the rest expressed no opinion.[11]

In answering questions framed in such a "use force or not" format, a respondent who wished to pressure Iraq to get out of Kuwait was seemingly offered only one way to accomplish the goal—war. Some respondents may have endorsed the choice being offered by pollsters even if it were not their own first choice. Had a method of pressuring Iraq short of war been offered, perhaps some would have chosen that instead.

Some other polls consistently found the American public narrowly divided on war in the Persian Gulf. These polls tended to pose the policy alternatives as "force versus continued sanctions." A *New York Times/CBS News* poll taken December 9 to December 11 asked, "If Iraq does not withdraw from Kuwait by January 15, do you think the U.S. should start military actions against Iraq, or should the U.S. wait longer to see if the trade embargo and other economic sanctions work?" The *Times* reported that 45 percent of Americans favored starting military action, 48 percent preferred to wait longer on sanctions, and 8 percent did not know.[12] A *USA Today* poll showed that 49 percent favored giving economic sanctions more time to work, 42 percent said the United States should attack, and 9 percent did not know.[13]

Polls using such a "force versus continued sanctions" format gave the impression of a split down the middle in the public's attitude toward going to war. Evidently, some respondents who wanted to see Iraq get out of Kuwait, and who might endorse war if that were the only option offered, preferred continuing the economic sanctions when that alternative was also presented.

That these seeming contradictions were actually the result of the different options offered by different pollsters and not other differences in each organization's methods, such as sampling procedures, dates of interviewing, or question ordering and context, is demonstrated by a few polls that managed to ask about war using *both* formats during the same interview.

A poll Gallup conducted December 6 and December 7 for *Newsweek* included both the "force or no force" format and the "force versus continued sanctions." Respondents were first asked, "Now that U.S. forces have been sent to Saudi Arabia and other areas of the Middle East, do you think they should engage in combat if Iraq refuses to leave Kuwait and restore its former government?" The *Newsweek* release reported that 56 percent of Americans said yes, and 33 percent said no; 11 percent did not know or had other responses. Just two questions later, respondents were asked, "Some people feel that President Bush should begin military action against Iraq soon after the January 15th United Nations deadline if Iraq has not withdrawn from Kuwait by then. Others say he should wait longer to see if economic and diplomatic sanctions are effective. Which comes closer to your view?" Only 41 percent backed military action, while 53 percent preferred waiting longer on sanctions and 6 percent expressed no opinion.[14]

Gallup conducted a similar experiment in two additional surveys—one taken from November 29 to December 2 and the other from December 6 to December 9. When favoring or opposing force were the only alternatives, 53 percent in each sampling favored "going to war with Iraq in order to drive the Iraqis out of Kuwait." But in each survey the public was narrowly split—in the same interview—when continued sanctions were posed as the alternative to war. "Some people feel the sanctions imposed by the international community against Iraq should be given more time to work. Other people feel that it is time to take stronger action against Saddam Hussein, including the use of armed force. Which one of these views comes closer to how you feel?" When it put the question that way, Gallup found 47 percent favored continued sanctions, 46 percent favored use of armed force, and 7 percent expressed no opinion in the December 6–9 interviews. In the November 29–December 2 interviews 46 percent favored continued sanctions, 48 percent armed force, and 6 percent expressed no opinion.

In a cross-tabulation supplied by Gallup from the December 6–9 interviews, 37 percent of the American public took a consistently hard line, favoring war over no war and force over continued sanctions (table 5-3). Another 30 percent took a consistently nonmilitary line, favoring no war over war and continued sanctions over force. These would appear to have been the two core bodies of opinion in the country. But together they totaled only two-thirds of Americans; the other third shifted between categories (and into and out of the "no opinion" category) according to which question was being asked. Of particular interest is that 14 percent of Americans favored going to war when sanctions were not an option but shifted away from force and favored sanctions once that choice was explicitly offered. Only 7 percent shifted the other way.

Table 5-3.   *Cross-Tabulation of Poll Respondents' Answers to Two Questions about Attitudes toward Use of Force in Kuwait, December 6–9, 1990*[a]

Percent of the entire sample (weighted numbers of respondents are in parentheses)

	War or no war[b]			
Force or sanctions[c]	Favor going to war	Oppose going to war	No opinion	Total
Force, stronger action	37	7	2	46
	(600)	(112)	(29)	(741)
Give sanctions time	14	30	3	47
	(219)	(486)	(54)	(759)
No opinion	2	3	2	7
	(37)	(52)	(30)	(119)
Total	53	40	7	100
	(855)	(651)	(114)	(1,020)

Source: Gallup Poll national telephone interviews of 1,007 adults, December 6–9, 1990. Cross-tabulation by Gallup. "Gallup News Service," wave 1, December 1990, pp. 37, 52.

a. Figures are weighted. Percentages are of entire sample. Order of first two row categories has been reversed from the order in the wording of the question for clearer presentation.

b. Column question: "If the current situation in the Middle East involving Iraq and Kuwait does not change by January, would you favor or oppose the U.S. going to war with Iraq in order to drive the Iraqis out of Kuwait?"

c. Row question: "Some people feel the sanctions imposed by the international community against Iraq should be given more time to work. Other people feel that it is time to take stronger action against Saddam Hussein, including the use of armed force. Which one of these views comes closer to how you feel?"

So, during December 1990 and January 1991 was the American public clearly in favor of going to war? Or were Americans seriously divided over which steps to take next to pressure Iraq? The answer, of course, is both. Each question format is limited and imperfect. In the end a close observer learns something valuable about the true state of public opinion by studying public responses to both formats.

When President Bush asked Congress in January 1991 for formal approval of the use of force in the Persian Gulf, the ensuing debate pitted advocates of force against advocates of continued sanctions. Those opinion polls that put the issue to the public as one of "force versus continued sanctions" had the merit of offering realistic alternatives that paralleled the options being considered in the formal debate in Washington. The consistently close public division in those polls underscored the importance of the congressional debate in helping the nation clarify and resolve the arguments over these alternatives.

But the majority for war obtained in response to the "force or no force" polling format also revealed the state of American public opinion. It showed what V. O. Key, Jr., called a "permissive consensus," a majority that was not demanding action but that would permit it and would support it once it took place.[15] This majority included many who held serious reservations. It was a majority, as events in subsequent months would show, that would rally in response to dramatic military events and leadership appeals but that throughout the crisis also had the potential to melt away if war proved to be lengthy, unsuccessful, or costly in American lives.

Looking beneath the Surface

Whichever format individual polling organizations chose to adopt, they best served their readers or viewers when they looked beneath the surface of their findings and tried to fathom the subtleties of public opinion. For instance, the willingness of many to wait longer on sanctions did not necessarily mean willingness to wait indefinitely. Some respondents who did not favor an immediate war may nonetheless have been reconciled to eventual combat. The *New York Times*/CBS News poll documented this point in finding that, in answer to a follow-up question, most of those favoring sanctions had in mind waiting only a few months for them to work, not waiting the year or more that some antiwar leaders were advocating. The poll, taken December 9–11, showed that half the people favoring sanctions were willing to wait three months beyond the January 15 deadline, but only one-fifth were willing to wait six months, and just one-sixth were willing to wait a year or longer.[16]

As another example, public willingness to use force did not necessarily mean desire for immediate war and an instant end to diplomatic effort. Some respondents who supported the use of force may nonetheless have been willing to wait awhile before attacking. The *Washington Post*/ABC News poll reported that, in answer to a follow-up question, the majority favoring war disagreed over timing. Only 39 percent who favored war wanted to attack immediately after the January 15 deadline, up from 29 percent in another *Washington Post*/ABC News poll a few days earlier. Another 43 percent favored using force "within a month," 12 percent said in "one to three months," and 2 percent said "four months or longer."[17]

Thus there was a certain convergence of polls and opinion. Many prowar people were willing to wait a bit, and many prosanctions people were unwilling to wait very long. However analyzed, the public's patience was clearly thin, and once the January 15 deadline passed without positive responses from Iraq, the patience was soon likely to run out entirely.

Leadership and Events Matter

The permissive majority willing to back force shot up to 70 or 80 percent after the bombs began to fall on January 16, 1991, according to polls from many organizations. Such a dramatic surge of support might surprise some observers if they expected the prewar levels to be permanent. But with the onset of actual hostilities the situation had fundamentally changed, and many Americans who initially opposed force now supported their troops overseas and their commander-in-chief in the White House, a phenomenon often called the rally-round-the-flag effect.[18]

The surge in support occurred immediately. On January 16, within hours of the start of the air war, Gallup found 81 percent of Americans approved the way President Bush was handling the situation, a rise of 19 percentage points from another Gallup poll earlier in the month. Gallup also found 79 percent saying they approved of the decision "to go to war with Iraq in order to drive the Iraqis out of Kuwait."[19]

A further demonstration is available from a panel study, conducted by the *New York Times* and CBS News, that interviewed the same respondents before and after the war began. Of 674 people who had been interviewed January 5–7, a total of 550 were interviewed again January 17–19. Between the two dates 29 percent of Americans shifted their views from waiting on sanctions to approving the start of military action (table 5-4).

Contingencies Also Matter

Once the air war began, polls started to assess support for a ground war—in case that was eventually necessary to force Iraq from Kuwait. During late January and the first half of February polls sometimes reached different conclusions about the likely level of support.

Those polls that provided the most careful picture engaged in some form of anticipatory analysis—for instance by showing that the level of support for a ground war was in part contingent upon the level of expected American casualties. Based on a *Wall Street Journal*/NBC News poll, conducted January 23, a week after the start of the air war, the *Journal* reported, "support for the war drops off sharply when voters confront the possibility of large casualties. While 75% say President Bush was right to attack when he did, support for continuing the war until U.S. objectives are met drops off to 56% when the prospect of 'thousands of American

Table 5-4.   *Cross-Tabulation of Same Poll Respondents' Answers to Questions Asked before and after Gulf War about Attitudes toward Military Actions against Iraq, January 5–7 and 17–19, 1991*[a]

Percent of completed panel (weighted numbers of respondents are in parentheses)

Interviewed after air war began[c]	Interviewed before air war began[b]			
	Start military action	Wait longer on sanctions	No opinion	Total
Right to start military action	44	29	4	78
	(242)	(160)	(24)	(427)
Should have waited longer on sanctions	2	15	*	18
	(13)	(85)	(2)	(100)
No opinion	1	2	1	4
	(6)	(11)	(5)	(22)
Total	48	47	6	100
	(261)	(257)	(31)	(549)

Source: *New York Times*/CBS News panel survey with national telephone interviews of 550 adults on January 5–7, 1991, before air war began, and January 1991, after air war began. "*New York Times*/CBS News Iraq Callback Poll A2," January 1991.

* Less than 0.5 percent.

a. Figures are weighted. Percentages are of entire sample.

b. Column question (before war): "The United Nations has passed a resolution authorizing the use of military force against Iraq if they do not withdraw their troops from Kuwait by January 15. If Iraq does not withdraw from Kuwait by then, do you think the United States should start military actions against Iraq, or should the United States wait longer to see if the trade embargo and other economic sanctions work?"

c. Row question (after war): "Do you think the United States did the right thing in starting military actions against Iraq, or should the United States have waited longer to see if the trade embargo and other economic sanctions worked?"

casualties' is mentioned; 38%, nearly four voters in 10, would favor a negotiated settlement to the conflict in that case."[20]

A January 4–6 *Washington Post*/ABC News poll showed that opposition to the use of force against Iraq rose from 32 percent to 53 percent "if it meant 1,000 American troops would be killed in the fighting," and rose further to 61 percent "if it meant 10,000 American troops would be killed in the fighting."[21]

In a February 12–13 *New York Times*/CBS News poll 60 percent initially said "the war to defeat Iraq is likely to be worth the loss of life and other costs." But that figure fell to 45 percent when reasked using the preamble, "suppose several thousand American troops would lose their lives in a ground war against Iraq."[22] Using another approach a Harris poll conducted February 8–10 found 80 percent of Americans favored ordering ground troops into battle, "if it is likely to involve light American casualties." But just 67 percent favored a ground battle that resulted in "moderate American casualties," and only 30 percent if there were "heavy American casualties."[23]

These anticipatory analyses gave a far different picture from the one given by polls that simply asked about attitudes toward a ground war. Pollsters as a profession were well prepared to conduct such analysis, since the widely known work of John Mueller and other scholars had demonstrated the impact of casualties on public support in both the Vietnam War and the Korean War.

The Rally at the Outbreak of the Ground War

Once the ground war began on February 23, 1991, another rally boosted President Bush's approval rating and propelled support for the ground assault into the 80 percent range. This surge paralleled the rallies in mid-January after the air war began and in early August 1990 when troops were initially dispatched to the Middle East, but it was especially intense because so many thousands of American troops were actually being sent into harm's way.

In a February 24 *New York Times*/CBS News poll 75 percent of respondents said the United States was "right to start the ground war," while 19 percent said it "should have waited longer to see if bombing worked." Earlier in February the proportions had been reversed: only 11 percent had wanted to begin the ground war soon, while 79 percent had preferred to continue bombing.[24] Thus many who were reluctant to approve of escalation in advance endorsed the policy after the fact (and after television broadcasts showed the swift success the ground assault was achieving).

Some observers might have been surprised at this dramatic variation in support if they assumed the levels of approval before the ground war were permanent.[25] But again, the situation to which the public was reacting had changed from a hypothetical military option fraught with uncertainty and danger to an actual ground assault that seemed to be going very well. To the rally-round-the-flag effect was added an understandable rally-round-success effect.

The February 24 *Washington Post*/ABC News poll likewise caught the rally and some of its causes: 80 percent of respondents said "it was right for the United States to begin a ground war now" and 49 percent said the war was going better than they had expected.[26]

Conclusion

The ground war required only one hundred hours and proved to be a rout with spectacularly few American casualties. Approval of President Bush immediately after the end of hostilities shot up to 88 percent in the

New York Times/CBS News poll, 89 percent in the Gallup poll, 90 percent in the *Washington Post*/ABC News poll, and 91 percent in the *USA Today* poll. The likely loss in support that was predicted if there were heavy U.S. casualties was never put to the test. But still any polls conducted before the ground war that failed to indicate the probable impact of heavy casualties were giving a simplistic picture of public opinion. Given the patterns observed in surveys during the Vietnam War and the Korean War, the permissive majority that was open to leadership by President Bush in late 1990 and early 1991 would probably have melted considerably if the war had been long and bloody.

The recent proliferation of national polls in the United States probably guarantees that some polling organizations will turn out to be more subtle or agile and others less so at any given moment. But proliferation also raises the odds that at least some organizations will indeed ask the right questions at the right time to probe beyond the immediate or temporary manifestations of American public opinion.

Polls on Domestic Issues

Although polls taken during political campaigns can vary in their results because of timing and question placement, and polls on foreign policy issues are particularly sensitive to dramatic events, leadership appeals, and how policy options are presented, one might expect that public opinion on domestic issues would be more solid, stable, and easier for pollsters to measure.

Certainly the public is more knowledgeable about domestic issues and familiar with their implications—particularly race relations, labor-management disputes, taxing and spending, and other longstanding matters. Americans have first-hand experience of these, and even a domestic issue that is seemingly new can often be fitted into some familiar mold, enabling people to see it as the latest instance of some ongoing controversy.

Nonetheless, polls on domestic issues do sometimes differ substantially in their findings, even for what appear to be familiar issues with well-drawn sides and highly visible protagonists. This is especially true of matters that involve multiple goals, clashing values, and other complexities that leave many citizens ambivalent or torn over the most desirable course for public policy. In such cases polls can register markedly different responses, depending on which aspects of a complex issue they emphasize in their questions. Different wordings can tap different values and trigger seemingly contradictory opinions, even from the same respondents during the same interview.

Whether a woman has a right to an abortion is an issue not unique in having such complexity, but it is particularly revealing. Surveys taken during 1989 offered fascinating examples of variability. Many polls on the subject were conducted that year because in July 1989 the Supreme Court ruled in *Webster* v. *Reproductive Health Services* to permit states to tighten restrictions on abortion, and several states attempted to do so. This energized both pro-life and pro-choice advocates to press their case, and each could find poll results to cite in claiming the public was on their side.

Multiple Questions When Values Conflict

Questions that emphasize a woman's freedom of choice usually elicit majority endorsement. Thus when asked whether a woman should be able to have an abortion if she wants it and her doctor agrees to it, six in ten Americans would allow an abortion.[27] If this were the only poll available, one would conclude that a solid majority of Americans is pro-choice. (This response may also be influenced by the invocation of medical authority in the phrase "and her doctor agrees to it.") But questions that emphasize the rights of the fetus also usually receive majority endorsement. For instance, when asked, "Which of these statements comes closer to your opinion—abortion is the same thing as murdering a child, or abortion is not murder because the fetus really isn't a child yet?" 50 percent typically choose the first response.[28] If that were the only poll result available, one might conclude that a majority of Americans is pro-life.

But the right to an abortion is more complex than either question suggests. In fact, it is so complex, and some Americans are so anguished about it, that they are capable of holding opposing views simultaneously. When those who say abortion is the same as murdering a child are asked the additional question "Do you agree or disagree with the following statement—abortion is sometimes the best course in a bad situation?" they frequently split into two almost equal size groups. As a result, in recent years from one-sixth to one-quarter of all Americans have said both that abortion is murder and that it is sometimes the best course.[29] This occurs because both a woman's freedom to control her own body and the sanctity of life (along with abhorrence of murder) are important values in American culture. Accordingly, any question about abortion that emphasizes one aspect to the neglect of the other will tell only part of the story.

The Inadequacy of "All or Nothing" Options

Questions that require them to choose between two extremes—unfettered access to abortion or complete abolition of abortion—place many Americans in an uncomfortable spot. Often those who would permit abortion still favor some types of restrictions, and many who are against abortion would still permit it in some situations. A question that allows a middle course—"Should abortion be legal as it is now, or legal *only* in such cases as rape, incest, or to save the life of the mother, or should it not be permitted at all?"—has in recent years elicited an average of 40 percent support for the current laws allowing abortion, 40 percent support for limiting abortion to the serious types of situations mentioned, and between 10 and 20 percent for outright prohibition.[30] Because of the large group in the middle, this distribution of opinion has allowed advocates on both sides of the issue to claim, respectively, that the vast majority of Americans want to restrict abortion or that the vast majority want abortion available.

When People Make Distinctions, Polls Should Too

That so many people approve of abortion but only under certain circumstances leads to speculation about other circumstances in which they might permit or disallow it. Since 1972 the annual General Social Survey, conducted by the National Opinion Research Center at the University of Chicago, has probed just such attitudes and has found repeatedly that people make clear distinctions between situations in which they think it should be possible for a pregnant woman to obtain a legal abortion and other situations in which they think it should not be possible.[31] In general, circumstances that involve a medical threat elicit a strong majority in favor of permitting abortion (table 5-5). This includes when the woman's own health is seriously endangered by the pregnancy, or when there is a strong chance of serious defect in the baby. Other serious situations, such as if a woman became pregnant as a result of rape, also elicit approval of abortion.

The public becomes much more divided when the reasons for abortion are mainly economic. Thus if a family has a very low income and cannot afford more children, the approval for abortion shrank to 46 percent. When the reason is mainly one of personal preference—if a woman is

Table 5-5.   *Distribution of Public Opinion on Allowing Abortion, by Circumstance of Pregnancy, General Social Survey, 1989*
Percent

	Abortion should be legal		
Woman's circumstance	Yes	No	Don't know
The woman's own health is seriously endangered by the pregnancy	88	10	2
The woman became pregnant as a result of rape	80	16	4
There is a strong chance of serious defect in the baby	78	18	3
The family has a very low income and cannot afford any more children	46	50	4
The woman is not married and does not want to marry the man	43	53	4
The woman is married and does not want any more children	43	54	4
The woman wants it for any reason	39	57	4

Source: *General Social Survey* (University of Chicago, National Opinion Research Center, July 1991). A small number of respondents who gave no answer is not shown. The question was, "Please tell me whether or not *you* think it should be possible for a pregnant woman to obtain a *legal* abortion if . . . ."

not married and does not want to marry the man— approval falls below 50 percent. When a woman wants an abortion "for any reason," support falls to 39 percent.

NORC surveys making such distinctions have been very influential, and a number of other polling organizations have extended research along the same lines, bringing the findings to an even wider audience. For example, a *Los Angeles Times* poll, taken March 3–10, 1989, tested seven similar sets of abortion circumstances, and reported similar patterns, as part of a one-hundred-question survey devoted entirely to attitudes toward abortion. A *New York Times*/CBS News July 1989 poll showed that people also made clear distinctions in other situations where a woman could be placed in a difficult situation by going through with a pregnancy. When the reasons might strike some respondents as more inconvenience than hardship—if the pregnancy would force a professional woman to interrupt her career—only 37 percent would permit abortion while 56 percent would disallow it. But when the consequences were more severe—if the pregnancy would force a teenage girl to drop out of school— 48 percent would allow abortion and 44 percent disallow it. And when a woman's motivation might strike respondents as overly casual or even frivolous—for example, when abortion is proposed as a substitute for other methods of birth control—a March 1989 *Los Angeles Times* poll found 80 percent opposed.

In April 1989 the *New York Times* constructed and displayed on its front page a "spectrum" of opinion on abortion from public reactions to five possible circumstances similar to those first posed by the General Social Survey—seriously endangered health of the mother, birth defect, low-income hardship, not wanting to marry the man, and pregnancy interfering with a woman's work or education. It showed that both pro-choice advocates and pro-life advocates are wrong in claiming that most of the public is on their side. Only 21 percent of Americans would permit abortion in every circumstance mentioned, and only 10 percent would forbid it in all five, while 70 percent of all Americans would allow abortion in some situations and oppose it in others.[32]

These patterns suggest that if people were offered additional opportunities to make even further distinctions regarding abortion, many might very well do so. When people want to make such distinctions, pollsters should too—if they are to give an accurate picture of public opinion.

Gauging Support for Policy on a Complex Subject

Measuring complex distinctions does not by itself suggest what policies the public would favor. When government policy is deliberated, still other values may come into consideration. If it were public policy to permit abortions only under certain circumstances, society might require some type of official tribunal to hear petitions, consider circumstances, and rule on individual cases. But Americans recoil from excessive government interference with private decisions. In a July 1989 *New York Times*/CBS News poll, 68 percent agreed "even in cases where I might think abortion is the wrong thing to do, I don't think the government has any business preventing a woman from having an abortion." A September 1989 *New York Times*/CBS News poll asked explicitly who should decide abortion cases: "If your state restricted the number of abortions performed, who should decide which women would be allowed to have abortions— the woman's own doctor, a doctor appointed by the state, a judge, or some state official?" An overwhelming 69 percent of the public preferred that a woman's own doctor make the decision. A March 1989 *Los Angeles Times* poll also documented the public belief that abortion should ultimately be a private decision: 74 percent of the respondents agreed that "I personally feel that abortion is morally wrong, but I also feel that whether or not to have an abortion is a decision that has to be made by every woman for herself."

Support for New Limitations

The critical center of American public opinion favors keeping abortion legally available but making an abortion harder to get. Thus majorities support some of the restrictions that have been debated in various states and enacted in some, such as Pennsylvania. In a March 1989 *Los Angeles Times* poll 83 percent of the respondents agreed that "minors should have to get their parents' permission before they get an abortion." In a September 1989 *New York Times*/CBS News poll, 83 percent favored "requiring that at least one parent be told before a girl under 18 years of age could have an abortion." Both findings suggest that the idea of parents' rights or family rights carries some weight with the public when it comes to abortion for minors.

Many would also support the sort of viability test that some state legislatures have considered. In a July 1989 *Los Angeles Times* poll, 57 percent favored "a test of viability to protect the unborn child; if it should be determined that the fetus could survive, then the abortion could not be performed." In a September 1989 *New York Times*/CBS News poll, 65 percent favored "in a pregnancy of 20 weeks or more, requiring a test to make sure that the fetus is not developed enough to live outside the womb before a woman could have an abortion." And, again, proposals that would require the consent of a medical authority—a disinterested professional presumably familiar with the facts of the woman's individual case—also traditionally elicit majority support.

Conclusion

The debate over the morality of abortion will not end soon, even if Supreme Court decisions alter the legal situation. In its June 1992 decision in *Planned Parenthood* v. *Casey*, the Court upheld the right to abortion by only five to four and allowed several limitations. If the laws do eventually change and mandate stricter limitations, there would be a new legal status quo and thus a different balance of advantages and disadvantages for both sides in the debate. But polls would still be needed to fathom the views of the public on the continuing clash of rights and values.

This discussion should be sufficient to make the observer beware of any poll that claims majority support for either side in the abortion debate based on a single question or a simplistic line of questioning. Multiple measures of sentiment are the recommended prescriptions for such a situation. If a particular poll fails to probe the subject in a sufficient variety of ways, then one has recourse to the large and growing body of polling data on abortion that is in the public domain. The recent proliferation of polls has helped build this body of data by contributing many approaches to the topic, many differently worded questions, and many nuances of analysis and interpretation.

Costs and Benefits of Proliferation

The proliferation of public opinion polls has entailed serious costs.

—The resulting potential for confusion is enormous. With so many polls available, advocates for any side of virtually any issue can find at least some poll to support their position.

—The impact of any one polling organization is reduced, including whichever organization one happens to consider the most responsible, conscientious, and wise.

—The credibility of all polls is potentially threatened, as some poll-watchers cynically conclude that none can be trusted.

But for the close observer, the proliferation is a boon. If two organizations reach discrepant findings on a particular subject, the odds are high that a third poll and a fourth will soon be released on the same subject. Such proliferation aids the observer in various ways.

—The public is no longer at the mercy of just one or two organizations as the sources of poll information.

—A close observer can see the consequence of differently worded questions or other variations in timing, method, and approach to the subject.

—Learning speeds up when new issues or unusual candidates arise and early polls treat them differently (and sometimes inadequately).

—Proliferation helps the observer to identify which findings seem to agree, to spot idiosyncratic polls more quickly, and to discount those findings that are flukes or blips.

No-fault variability in methods, variability that happens without any evidence of error, shoddiness, or methodological sin, is actually useful in that it allows our understanding of public opinion to rest on more than one approach. When there were fewer polls available, results from two organizations that seemed contradictory were often not resolved until long afterward, if at all. Thus the recent proliferation of polls also helps to create its own check. In short, a multiplicity of somewhat different polls and divergent approaches allows the self-correcting tendencies of the survey profession to assert themselves faster than they would without such pluralism.

A Countervailing Trend

That the proliferation of national polls has strong benefits that outweigh the costs is underscored by a recent countervailing development in one type of polling. Since 1990 there have been fewer election day exit polls because ABC, CBS, CNN, and NBC pooled resources to create Voter Research & Surveys. Instead of competing with one another, they commissioned VRS to conduct a single polling operation on their behalf. They also invited national newspapers to subscribe to the service, with the condition that the papers would have only limited influence over the service.

As a consequence, instead of having available several independent efforts to explore the voters' minds, the observer of polls in 1990 suddenly had only one network-sponsored exit poll. Many observers criticized such "reverse proliferation," although it was perhaps inevitable given the financial straits of the networks, because it reduced the variety of data available for primary as well as secondary analysis and eliminated potential checks on erroneous conclusions. A reduction from three competing exit polls to one means less variability in topics and question wording, in methods, and therefore in results. It instantly solves the problem of discrepant findings, but at the cost of making it much more difficult to spot misleading findings that stem from sampling flukes, effects of question wording, or other decisions that go into any polling effort. And in at least one important instance already it has meant a lack of any data at all: in Pennsylvania's special election for U.S. senator in November 1991, no exit poll was conducted to record the psychology and demography of the electorate in Democrat Harris Wofford's upset victory over Republican Richard Thornburgh (widely attributed to support for Wofford's proposal of national health care).[33]

In defense of VRS, it has made available to its participating networks the possibility of "unilateral questions"— exclusive questions devised and paid for by an individual network and fielded by VRS in addition to its common polling effort. CBS News commissioned enough such questions in 1990 to form an entire second questionnaire distributed in VRS's sample precincts. The *New York Times* cooperated with CBS News in designing and sharing part of the cost for these additional questions, which explored many topics not included in the common VRS questionnaire and used differently worded questions to cover some topics that were included in both. This precedent leaves open the possibility that in the future the networks will still be able to contribute valuable different perspectives to exit polling even within the VRS framework.[34]

Looking at the Preponderance

If this chapter offers one dominant piece of advice it is this: keep an eye on what a majority of the polls are finding on any given topic, and weigh what findings seem to be in common. That advice should serve the observer well over the long run.

Although observers may find they sometimes have to struggle to discern the true outlines of public opinion from a multiplicity of polls, they still enjoy the decided advantage of a plurality of data. And they have an additional advantage when they know what to look for as they confront and try to capitalize on the rich resources of poll data that are available.

Notes

1. "Dukakis's Lead Drops to Pre-Convention Levels," *Gallup Report*, no. 276 (September 1988), p. 2.

2. Louis Harris and Associates survey 842110, July 20–24, 1984, summarized in an internal Harris staff memo, July 30, 1984.

3. Michael R. Kagay, "In Judging Polls, What Counts Is When and How Who Is Asked What," *New York Times*, September 12, 1988, p. A16.

4. One survey, the NBC News/*Wall Street Journal* poll, is based solely on registered voters, even in nonelection years and when its topics are unconnected with politics.

5. For a discussion of pursuit procedures, see Marjorie Connelly, Janet Elder, and Deborah Hofmann, "Refusals in Telephone Surveys: Persuading Respondents to Reconsider and the Effects of Conversions on Results," paper prepared for the 1990 annual meeting of the American Association for Public Opinion Research.

6. Michael R. Kagay, "The Use of Public Opinion Polls by *The New York Times*: Some Examples from the 1988 Presidential Election," in Paul J. Lavrakas and Jack K. Holley, eds., *Polling and Presidential Election Coverage* (Newbury Park, Calif.: Sage Publications, 1991), pp. 44–45.

7. See Irving Crespi, *Pre-Election Polling: Sources of Accuracy and Error* (Russell Sage Foundation, 1988).

8. After the 1980 presidential election the *New York Times* and CBS News conducted the second wave of a panel survey in which respondents to the final preelection poll were reinterviewed. They were asked whether they had voted as they had earlier said they intended to and, if not, why not. The results showed a net shift of 7 percentage points in Reagan's favor caused by changes in both voter preference and higher nonvoting rates

among Carter supporters. See Adam Clymer, "Poll Shows Iran and Economy Hurt Carter among Late-Shifting Voters," *New York Times*, November 16, 1980, p. A1.

9. Crespi, *Pre-Election Polling.*

10. Richard Morin, "Public Supports Move for Talks, But Most Doubt U.N. Vote will Compel Iraqi Pullout," *Washington Post*, December 4, 1990, pp. A27, A29.

11. Gerald F. Seib and Michel McQueen, "Poll Finds Americans Feel Hawkish toward Iraq But Would Grant Some Concessions to Avoid War," *Wall Street Journal*, December 13, 1990, p. A16.

12. Michael Oreskes, "Poll Finds Americans Divided on Sanctions or Force in Gulf," *New York Times*, December 14, 1990, pp. A1, A14.

13. Paul Clancy, "Poll: National Split on Iraq War," *USA Today*, December 3, 1990, p. 1A.

14. *Newsweek Poll*, press release December 8, 1990, pp. 3-4.

15. V. O. Key, Jr., *Public Opinion and American Democracy* (Knopf, 1961), pp. 32–35.

16. "*New York Times*/CBS News Poll, December," December 9-11, 1990.

17. Richard Morin, "Poll: Americans Expect War but Back Peace Conference," *Washington Post*, January 11, 1991, p. A1.

18. John E. Mueller, *War, Presidents and Public Opinion* (John Wiley, 1973), p. 53. A very thorough roundup of poll results in the early part of the Persian Gulf crisis is Rosita M. Thomas, *American Public Opinion on the Iraq-Kuwait Crisis until January 15* (Congressional Research Service, 1991).

19. "Buildup to War," *Gallup Poll Monthly* (January 1991), p. 17.

20. Michel McQueen, "Polled Americans Strongly Support Gulf War, Even Beyond Goals of U.N. Mandate on Kuwait," *Wall Street Journal*, January 25, 1991, p. A14.

21. Richard Morin, "Gulf Poll: Most Americans Want Hill to Back Bush," *Washington Post*, January 8, 1991, p. A12.

22. Maureen Dowd, "Americans Back Continued Air Strikes," *New York Times*, February 15, 1991, p. A15.

23. "Public Opposes Sending U.S. Troops into Ground Battles If Casualties Will Be 'Heavy,'" Harris poll, February 17, 1991.

24. Michael R. Kagay, "Public Shows Support for Land War," *New York Times*, February 26, 1991, p. A17.

25. Some editors on the foreign desk at the *New York Times* initially reacted with much amusement (and in some cases friendly derision) when I reported this apparent flip-flop.

26. Richard Morin, "Backing for War, Bush Role Grows with Ground Attack," *Washington Post*, February 26, 1991, p. A6.

27. In four *New York Times*/CBS News surveys in January, April, and July 1989, for example, support ranged between 58 and 63 percent. "*New York Times*/CBS News Poll September Survey," September 17–20, 1989.

28. In six surveys by *New York Times* and CBS News between 1983 and 1989, agreement ranged between 40 and 57 percent, averaging 50 percent. "*New York Times*/CBS News Poll," September 17–20, 1989.

29. In three 1989 polls the *New York Times* and CBS News found that 16 to 21 percent held both views, down from 26 percent in 1985. "*New York Times*/CBS News Poll," September 17–20, 1989.

30. The *New York Times* and CBS News measured this view thirteen times between 1985 and 1989 and found these proportions very stable. "*New York Times*/CBS News Poll," September 17–20, 1989.

31. The findings from 1972 to 1988 are available in Richard G. Niemi, John Mueller,

and Tom W. Smith, *Trends in Public Opinion: A Compendium of Survey Data* (Westport, Conn.: Greenwood Press, 1989), pp. 201–13. The 1989 results are in *General Social Survey July* (University of Chicago, National Opinion Research Center, 1991).

32. "Abortion Attitudes: Case by Case" [figure], *New York Times*, April 26, 1989, p. A1. The poll results showed 21 percent would allow abortion in *all* five circumstances; 15 percent would allow abortion in four of the five; 12 percent would allow abortion in three of the five; 26 percent would allow abortion in two of the five; 17 percent would allow abortion in one of the five; and 10 percent would allow abortion in *none* of the five circumstances. This "spectrum of acceptance" accompanied E.J. Dionne, Jr.'s, article, "Poll on Abortion Finds the Nation Is Sharply Divided."

33. Although no exit poll was conducted, a postelection statewide telephone poll designed by Robert J. Blendon of the Harvard School of Public Health and conducted by KRC Communications Research, Newton, Mass., for the Henry J. Kaiser Family Foundation documented the impact of the health care issue on voters' decisions. Summarized in Robert J. Blendon, "Poll Shows National Health Insurance as Pivotal Issue in Pennsylvania Senate Race," Henry J. Kaiser Family Foundation, Menlo Park, Calif., November 7, 1991.

34. Statewide exit polls are occasionally conducted by non-network agencies, most notably over the years by the *Los Angeles Times*, but exit polling (and particularly nationwide exit polling) has always been mainly a creature of network television news.

Chapter 6

The Impact of Media Polls on the Public

MICHAEL W. TRAUGOTT

N EWS ORGANIZATIONS' use of polls has increased dramatically in the past twenty years. With this "proliferation" of polls, as some have called it, has come greater concern from social scientists, political commentators, and media critics that the reporting of poll results has harmfully influenced the electorate. Many feel that the number of polls or the use of polls or the reporting of polls by news organizations is excessive.[1] But content analysis studies produce different results depending on how such concepts are measured and which media are analyzed. Still, by the 1988 presidential election, public exposure to news reports based on polls was widespread; and critics warned that both pre-election polls and election night projections of winners affected elections. This chapter reviews theories and models of polling effects, empirical studies that support or refute them, and commentary on the effects of polls in contemporary campaigns.

Assessments of the impact of media polls on the electorate are complicated by the range of effects that might occur, including increased or decreased levels of political interest, knowledge about candidates or issues, and increased support for one candidate or another. Assessments are also complicated by considerations of whether the effects would occur among the public, political elites, or both. Polls may increase support for the underdog or create a bandwagon for the leading candidate. The pub-

Partial support for the preparation of this paper was provided by the Program in Media and Politics at the Center for Political Studies, University of Michigan. I wish to thank Bhavin Shah and Elisabeth Traugott for research assistance.

lication of poll results before an election could stimulate turnout when the outcome is in doubt or depress it when there is a clear favorite. And election night projections of likely presidential winners before the polls have closed everywhere in the United States may affect those who vote late in the day.

After all the evidence is reviewed, it is difficult to escape the conclusion that media polls do affect the public. Reports of poll results, especially of the relative standing of the candidates, influence all kinds of attitudes and behavior in the electorate. Among political elites, including financial backers of candidates, campaign staff, consultants, and even journalists, the effects are relatively easily observable and well understood. Money flows to candidates whose electability seems likely according to the polls, for example, and quantities of news coverage track well with standings in the polls before any primaries are even held. These responses are as likely to be based on public polls reported by news organizations as on private polls that candidates flaunt for strategic purposes.

Less obvious and less well understood are the effects on individual citizens, which may include their preferences among candidates, whether they turn out to vote, and, of course, how they vote. Serious problems associated with the research designs necessary to demonstrate these effects conclusively will probably never be surmounted because of the costs and other resources that would be required. Therefore it is necessary to rely on available evidence to suggest the nature and magnitude of likely effects.

One problem in measuring the impact of polls on the public and the democratic process is that so many of the effects are indirect. If a potential candidate never formally challenges an incumbent because published polls show any challenger would have to overcome a 20-percentage-point deficit in voter appeal, or if a potential contributor never writes a check to support a candidate because the polls show the candidate is far behind, the information can be said to have had a significant effect on a race. But it is difficult to describe this as a direct effect on the public when a candidacy never gets off the ground. Only in a general election campaign when the actual pairing of candidates is known can direct effects of polls usually be observed—in the form of stimulated turnout, for example. However, the impact of polls on the structure and the dynamics of a particular race could be greatest in determining the actual pairing in a contest—whether an incumbent faces a strong or weak challenger.

Of equally great concern, the reporting of survey results and their use to focus on which candidate is ahead or behind has led some to suggest that media polls harm democracy. The horse race emphasis conditions the electorate to evaluate candidates in terms of their electability instead of their positions on issues. And increasingly vocal segments of society feel that the frequent reporting of candidate standings, especially late in the campaign, diminishes the value of their vote and represents an intrusion into the electoral process. Reports of a consensus about who is likely to win denigrates a concept held by many citizens that their voting decision is private. For some their decision seems to be contaminated by the extensive information about how others are deciding.

These popular feelings and the implicit threat to regulate the reporting of poll results conflict with news organizations' First Amendment right to collect and disseminate information and their self-described goal of ensuring an informed electorate.[2] The media argue that the public's right to know supersedes considerations of whatever effect a poll may have on the electorate or on some candidates' chances of winning, even when election night coverage is involved.[3] For journalists, the solution to this dilemma, short of a news blackout that would not unduly discriminate against the networks, would be to have everyone vote at the same time and to close the polls simultaneously. This conflict in values, originally embodied in concerns about the networks' election night projections but now extending to concerns about the more general use of polls by the media, is affecting public evaluations of pollsters and news organizations' campaign coverage, with the possibility that overall confidence in media organizations might suffer as well.[4]

The problem of horse race journalism is most serious in a two-candidate race, given our winner-take-all electoral system. But the three-way contest in the 1992 presidential campaign presented an unusual opportunity for strategic voting. In order for citizens to value their vote in terms of the chances of their first choice and their least preferred candidate, they have to know the relative standing of the candidates. And poll results can provide such information.

Problems in Understanding the Effects of Polls

Evaluating the effects of media polls on the public is complicated by a lack of agreement as to just what those effects might be. As is so often the case in studies of mass communications, the indirect consequences of exposure are as important as the direct effects. Research has also been complicated by the counterbalancing occurrence of simultaneous effects. Whenever research is conducted on as large a group as the presidential electorate, for example, there are bound to be effects that push some subgroups one way and pull others in a different direction. In the aggregate there may often be little measurable net effect. Careful research designs and sophisticated data analysis techniques are needed to isolate small but meaningful shifts among subsamples.

Hypotheses about the impact of media polls conform to researchers' general expectations about the effects of information on the electorate: after all, media polls represent a special case of information dissemination during a campaign. However, there are three important points about possible effects of media polls that need to be emphasized because they can cause confusion in evaluating results from multiple studies. First, the effects may be indirect as well as direct, which makes assessing their consequences that much more difficult. Second, although critics' expressions of concern suggest that the effects of polls are overwhelmingly bad, the introduction of empirically based information about candidates and their campaigns has improved the quality of news coverage in many ways and thereby benefited the electorate. This includes reporting the relative standing of candidates. Finally, any discussion of the impact of polls cannot be completely divorced from considerations of the stage of a campaign at which the information becomes available to the public. At different points in the campaign, members of the electorate can be characterized by different levels of attentiveness, interest, and self-described needs for information. Defining the range of possible effects has to take into account these characteristics of members of the audience as well as when they are exposed to polling information.

Direct and Indirect Effects

The effects of polls are not limited to members of the general public during an election campaign. Polls can influence political elites as well.[5] Most financial contributors, for example, want to back a winner. Results from media polls, as well as private polls paid for by a campaign, are commonly used by candidates to encourage support for their efforts or to discourage contributions to an opponent who, they would argue, has little chance of winning. These effects can be especially pronounced early in the campaign, when candidates are often not well known and not rated highly in polls.

Harrison Hickman has identified several factors that may contribute to the impact of polls on the electorate: citizens' orientation to candidates and campaigns, especially their evaluations of whether a candidate is viable; the availability of information other than poll results; the urgency of making a prompt decision; the strength of commitment to a candidate; and an initial predisposition to a given candidate.[6] These considerations are tempered by people's trust in polls for information. The interpretation of poll results is never left solely to the electorate; campaigns always provide a spin that puts their candidates in the best possible light.

Poll results also carry particular weight for political activists.[7] Profes sional campaign staff workers who are trying to decide which campaign to join, and whose careers are often based on their record of working for successful campaigns, use the results to evaluate candidates' chances. Volunteers may also use them to decide which candidate to help. A poor showing in the polls can devastate a nascent candidacy, especially of someone who is qualified but relatively unknown, if it limits fund-raising possibilities and campaign staffing.

Further into a presidential campaign, polls are used to evaluate popular reactions to possible vice presidential nominees. The results, which are very sensitive to how questions are phrased and ordered and are subject to wildly varying interpretations, affect potential nominees as well as convention delegates.[8] Although the presidential nominees will exert the most influence on the delegates' selection of running mates, they will have seen public and private polls on favored vice presidential nominees. And immediately after the convention, polls may assess the contribution of vice presidential nominees to the ticket. This was clearly the case in 1984 with Representative Geraldine Ferraro, when polls were used to evaluate the effects of her selection on the gender gap, and in 1988 with Senators Dan Quayle and Lloyd Bentsen, when polls assessed the public's sense of their suitability to serve as president. Quayle's problems with public evaluations in the polls continued in 1992. These kinds of poll results contribute to journalists' handicapping of each party's team.

The dissemination of polling information during the campaign or on election night may also produce apathy among party workers, either be- cause their candidate is so far ahead or so far behind. This is the equivalent of the closeness hypothesis that suggests that the value of a vote is greater when the outcome of the race is in doubt. Therefore, eagerness to help, as well as eagerness to vote, increases when polls show a tight race and decreases when the outcome seems inevitable.

Potential Benefits and Drawbacks of Polls

The dissemination of polling results during a campaign is not always harmful to democracy or to members of the electorate. For every so-called negative effect—with the exception of false or inaccurate information—there is at least in principle a compensating benefit. The actual or expected effects have as much to do with the circumstances of a particular election and the media's treatment of specific poll results as they do with the people exposed to the information.

For example, a basic function of the press during a political campaign is to supply the electorate with information on which to base judgments about candidates. Poll results can provide people with more and better information about who is running, the dynamics of their campaigns, and the popular response to their positions on issues. This would be especially true if news organizations placed less emphasis on reporting who is winning.

Polls that show a close contest can increase interest in an election and persuade people that their vote can help determine the outcome.[9] The results of private and public polls even could help political parties select better candidates, given that the best way for parties to participate in governing is to select candidates who have the greatest chance of winning elections.[10]

The American electoral system is heavily stacked in favor of the two major parties. However, presidential primaries are multicandidate contests, and occasionally a general election campaign will feature a relatively serious third-party candidate. In the 1992 campaign, for instance, poll results can supply important information to strategic voters in primaries—those who want to maximize the long-run success of their preferred candidate. In a primary or caucus they might vote for a less preferred candidate so as to affect the order of finish and preserve their preferred candidate's options in a later contest.

The 1992 election provides an interesting perspective on an independent candidacy in the general election. Ross Perot generated substantial public support without entering any primaries. In fact, he is the only independent candidate ever to lead two major-party candidates in pre-election polls. But in general elections many citizens become concerned about wasting their vote and abandon their first choice in favor of a candidate who has a reasonable chance to win. Poll results can show relative standings of preferred candidates and opponents, information not available from other sources. The candidates themselves are likely to use this same information to make their pitch to voters.

Despite these potential benefits, critics assume that most of the effects of polls are harmful. If polls are poorly conducted, problems with accuracy or bias can arise, and the reported results may mislead the public. Publication of results showing one candidate far ahead may have a depressing effect on turnout, labeled a slack effect or an abstention effect.[11] This may be true whether one candidate's advantage is known well before election day or is learned only through early projections of outcomes on election night. The dissemination of poll results may also affect voters' choices of candidates.[12] Showing that one candidate is far ahead may cause a band-wagon effect, drawing additional supporters, or an underdog effect, by sending sympathetic voters to a weaker opponent. Each of these persistent concerns represents a very difficult challenge for researchers.

Polling Effects and Campaign Phases

Voters respond to different phases of a presidential campaign in different ways. Before the nominations the public shows less interest in the candidates and participates less in campaigns. Because party identification is not a useful cue in the primaries, people have come to rely on news media campaign coverage to tell them who the candidates are, what they stand for, and what their electoral prospects are. The use of polls in this coverage is common and is bound to have some effect on public perceptions. The amount of coverage that candidates receive has been related to their relative standing in the polls and vice versa.[13] Voters' assessments of candidates are heavily influenced by perceptions of viability and electability.[14] And candidates' levels of recognition and their momentum are clearly linked to patterns of horse race coverage.[15]

The information sources available during presidential primaries are diverse, and most people use more than one source.[16] Although talking with family and friends is not often mentioned as a main source of political information, people have estimated they obtained one-third of their information this way. Some may scan the news especially for information that can be used in these conversations. Because candidate standing dominates coverage and may be just such a useful topic, people may focus inadvertently on poll-based news coverage.

Researchers have identified important effects of media polls during the general election campaign as well and have assessed how strong they are and whether they change during the course of the campaign. Earlier explanations of voting behavior were based primarily on party identification and other supposed enduring and stable factors.[17] More recent research has focused on the proposed categorizing of voters into precampaign deciders and late deciders. A significant group of voters who are not interested in a campaign before it starts may pay "close attention to the heavy flow of information during the campaign and vote on the basis of this information."[18] The size of this group may be larger and more volatile in closely fought campaigns. The characteristics of people who vote at various times of the day may also differ; it is possible that "potentially more influenceable voters tend to cast their ballots somewhat later in the day than the rest of the electorate."[19] Of course, one of the things that could influence them at the last minute would be media projections of a winner.

A special but infrequent circumstance in American presidential elections is the appearance of third-party candidates on the ballot: the most recent serious candidates have been George Wallace in 1968, John Anderson in 1980, and Ross Perot in 1992. All were faced with demonstrating their viability or electability, a problem analogous to that faced by primary candidates. But in the general election campaign, people are more likely to be concerned about wasting their votes. One of the main cues potential supporters of third-party candidates have is their choice's standing in the polls. A drop in popularity can change perceptions of them from serious candidates to spoilers who have no chance of winning; and their support can wither accordingly.

News organizations have increasingly used polls to gauge the public's reactions to debates and its evaluations of the participants. During the 1980 campaign, pollsters even asked whether John Anderson should be included in debates, and his standing in major national polls became a criterion for inclusion. The use of polls to determine the winners of debates is another form of horse race journalism adapted to a special event during a campaign. Therefore, the effects can more usefully be seen as indirect. Determinations of who won a debate can alter public perceptions about which candidate is more viable or electable, and that in turn can affect voter preference. These effects can be equally significant in primary campaigns.

News organizations began routinely conducting polls to evaluate debate participants as a way to distance themselves from the spin or interpretation conferred by candidates and their staffs. In the 1976 coverage, "one re-

current theme, largely based on polls but also expressed in private estimates, was that Ford had 'won' the first debate. . . . The difference
could be designated a 'polling effect' but is more correctly a reflection of
the overall image conveyed by the media."[20] The perception of a winner
is thus determined mostly by information from sources other than the
direct experience of watching a debate itself. Previous preferences seem
to guide immediate judgments, but media interpretations after a debate
may sway voters away from this immediate partisan division.[21]

Although news descriptions of the outcomes of debates affect popular
perceptions of the candidates, the effects may be transitory and are more
likely to influence less politically involved members of the electorate than
strong partisans. Consistent with the rest of their campaign coverage,
news organizations increasingly use polls to assess the winners of debates,
especially as part of subsequent analysis. With careful advance preparation, television networks have been able to report preliminary poll results
an hour after a debate. These results can frame assessments of candidates
for a changeable and undecided segment of the population and affect the
outcome of close races.

Polls and Voter Preference

The direct effects of polls are usually said to be changes in voter
preferences for candidates and in propensities to turn out on election day.
A close contest can stimulate interest; knowing that one candidate has a
seemingly insurmountable lead can dampen it. Most voters are steadfast
in supporting a candidate, either out of partisanship or because of their
satisfaction with an incumbent. For a few, however, jumping on a leader's
bandwagon supplants a more deliberate and rational evaluation of two
opponents, just as for some others a sympathetic response to a trailing
candidate has the same effect.

In competitive races, changes in the preferences of a relatively few
voters can often determine outcomes. Such changes might reflect considered opinion based on careful examination of available information, or
they might represent a whimsical response to chance exposure to new
information by voters with lightly held attitudes and little commitment
to candidates. These reactions suggest quite different potential effects of
news content, including polls, on voters.

Early studies of voter reaction found stable patterns of preference that
were strongly influenced by party identification. But with weakening

partisanship and greater exposure to more sophisticated candidate appeals, voter volatility appears to have increased, as has the proportion of those who decide late in a campaign. Voters who change their allegiance are likely to be of higher socioeconomic status and, especially, have more education, which makes them susceptible to media influences. Late deciders have been people with little political involvement or partisanship, and media effects on them seem to have been substantial as well.[22]

Perceptions of what others are thinking may also affect a person's attitudes. Studies in West Germany have suggested that an individual's fear of isolation could alter opinions in some circumstances in which change is possible, and election campaigns are certainly such a case. This formulation is not so much a consistent variation on the bandwagon effect as it is an explanation for why people usually do not flock to underdogs. Bandwagon effects are most likely to occur late in a campaign, but the "spiral of silence," when people are reluctant to express support for a position or candidate they believe does not have wide support among others, is most likely to be strongest early, when many people hold opinions lightly and are most ready to respond to others' opinions.[23]

Researchers tested this idea with a small panel of voters who were interviewed at three points during the 1976 presidential campaign, one in which there was no clear favorite. They found that judgments of what others believed (estimated public support for Gerald Ford or Jimmy Carter and how it was changing) affected voter preference, particularly for those respondents who demonstrated ambivalence or uncertainty.[24] Polls provide an obvious indication of how others are evaluating the candidates and could form the basis for such judgments.

Although most of the interest in the effects of poll results focuses on the distribution of voter preference, important questions have been raised about effects on turnout. A close election would be expected to stimulate turnout; reports of a lopsided majority would depress it. Both views result from citizens' assessments of the value of their votes in determining the outcome of an election and hence the expected utility from participating.[25] Again, the research results are mixed.

A study of the effects of election night broadcasts in 1964 found a decreased eagerness to vote on the part of those who had learned of Lyndon Johnson's probable landslide victory and for whom this was an unexpected result. But the decreased interest was the same for supporters of Barry Goldwater, for whom the size of the loss might have been more unexpected. The study observed that the greatest effects on turnout are likely to be found as people become certain of the outcome, find their expectations invalidated by the returns, or see their own candidate as the underdog.[26]

An experiment conducted among Indiana University undergraduates registered to vote for the first time focused on how manipulated information about the expected outcome of the 1972 presidential race affected voter preference, the estimated value of voting, and eagerness to vote. Respondents were given information about expected victory margins for Richard Nixon and George McGovern that were the same as they had anticipated or greater or smaller. For initial McGovern supporters, but not Nixon supporters, larger Nixon margins influenced preferences, the value of voting, and eagerness to vote. In particular, when the Nixon margin increased, the eagerness of McGovern supporters to vote declined. The study concluded that in a one-sided presidential election, supporters of the trailing candidate may become less intense and less motivated to vote after they have been exposed to in-state election poll reports.[27]

A recent panel study also found a weakening of intentions to vote when registered voters, interviewed before and after the 1988 presidential race, were told of George Bush's lead in the polls. One in ten of the small group of nonvoting registrants volunteered that "their expectation of a George Bush victory influenced their decision not to vote." A similar proportion thought this expectation "may" have contributed to their not voting.[28]

But other researchers have been unable to reproduce these results in the context of local elections using a postelection survey of known nonvoters drawn from registration rolls. When respondents were asked why they did not vote, few cited advance knowledge of the outcome based on polls. No one volunteered this reason in response to an open-ended question; and selecting from a list of possible reasons, only 20 percent said polls reporting that the candidates they liked were far ahead or behind was at least "somewhat important."[29] The authors concluded that preelection publication of poll results showing lopsided majorities had little effect.

Accuracy, Bias, and Misinformation

Concerns about poorly collected, inaccurate, or poorly interpreted data have been raised by pollsters and their critics since the 1930s and have increased when the performance of preelection polls has faltered.[30] Some observers complain that careful attention to survey methods occurs only during high-visibility presidential campaigns.[31] Early in the campaign, when some candidates are relatively unknown, journalists may find themselves asking readers or viewers to discount poll results, while they organize their entire coverage of the general election campaign around the latest findings. Unsophisticated consumers of this kind of information may wonder whether polls are worth anything at all.

Polling data are directed to various audiences, but only a few readers and viewers can be expected to understand the conditions under which the data have been collected and the limitations on interpretation that may result. Despite the efforts of the American Association for Public Opinion Research and the National Council of Public Polls to promulgate disclosure standards, most consumers are unaware of the methodological details of polling. The audience's interpretive task is complicated even more by news organizations that cosponsor data collection but publish differing interpretations of the results. For example, in the 1988 presidential campaign the *Washington Post* and ABC News sponsored a survey data collection effort covering all fifty states. The data collection methodologies and the timing of the surveys varied greatly from state to state, and the organizations' extrapolations from the survey results led to differing estimates of the electoral vote support for Bush and Dukakis.[32]

Even though most people do not understand the statistical principles under which polls are conducted, they believe that pollsters are doing a good job.[33] Thus the use of some techniques such as probability sampling can give stories based on polls greater credibility. But although confidence in polling remains high, attitudes toward the reporting of who is ahead are a different story. In a 1988 Gallup survey, 38 percent of respondents indicated such reporting was a "good thing," but 45 percent believed it was a "bad thing." And 47 percent believed that reporting who is ahead "does not improve coverage" (38 percent believed it does).[34] Public sentiment was distinctly more negative about election night projections of winners: 70 percent believed that television networks should not report the projections because it discourages voting.

Bandwagon and Underdog Effects

The problem of potential bandwagon and underdog effects has shadowed pollsters since the advent of their business. The dilemma is essentially an ethical one. Does publishing the results of a poll affect the very attitudes and opinions being measured and intrude on the democratic process? "In a democratic election the purpose of the secret ballot is presumably twofold. One function is the protection of the voter's anonymity, and the other is the preclusion of influence of the marked ballot upon the unmarked. In a sense, the more valid the procedures for the prediction of elections become, the nearer such polls approximate reports of the summation of the secret ballots of the entire electorate."[35] Even in the 1940s, the pervasiveness of media reports based on polls meant that most Americans were aware of them and trusted them.[36] The prominence of polls has since increased as news organizations themselves have collected data and promoted the results. So the possible existence of bandwagon and underdog effects has become increasingly important.

Predictably, those who have a commercial interest in seeing the polling industry prosper have argued that bandwagon and underdog effects do not occur. As early as 1940 the Gallup organization noted that candidates' leads in surveys tended to decrease as election day got closer. Although this argument was frequently cited by other pollsters, it was not demonstrated empirically to be conclusive.[37]

Establishing the existence of bandwagon and underdog effects is as difficult as any research task in communications. The problem is to understand a citizen's initial attitude or behavioral predisposition, to know that he or she was exposed to news content containing polling information, and then to ascertain whether a change in attitudes or behavior has taken place because of that exposure. Ideally this problem would be overcome as plausible alternative explanations for observed changes were eliminated. But analyzing bandwagon and underdog effects is complicated by the likelihood that they could occur simultaneously and might vary among different segments of the electorate. In the aggregate, they could cancel each other out or result in such a small net effect as to appear statistically insignificant.

Problems of validity also arise because of the populations studied and the contexts in which they are studied. Experimental settings are the best way to study bandwagon and underdog effects, but research on students or in nonpolitical contests makes applying the results to the general electorate difficult. The settings may, for example, show that exposure to others' attitudes results in increased conformity.[38] Reference groups or the concept of a reference public have been used to explain why such effects might occur. But readers of poll results may not see survey respondents as members of the same group of voters that they themselves belong to.

One reason for persistent concern about the effects of preelection polls on voters' choices is that postelection responses reflect bandwagon effects on reported votes, so preelection bandwagon effects could exist as well. Such a view is based on the idea that "the most authentic statement of majority opinion [is] the results of the election."[39] If some citizens respond after the fact in a way that suggests they have adjusted their attitudes or reported behavior to conform to the outcome of the election, why wouldn't some, especially in the context of pervasive credible polling information, adjust their behavior before the election?[40]

One of the earliest reported studies of the effects of public opinion on voter preferences was also one of the more sophisticated in design and analysis. In an experiment, researchers demonstrated a bandwagon effect among students who were told the results of a *Literary Digest* poll. In a second experiment that attempted to replicate the first, the researchers observed relationships in the expected direction, but the results were not statistically significant given the sample sizes. In a warning to subsequent researchers, they concluded that "future studies to test the bandwagon theory by the practical method of the straw ballot must be prepared to use fairly large samples."[41]

The most complete and fully elaborated design for a bandwagon study, although the project was never carried out, proposed a geographically based experiment in which neighborhood or precinct-level opinion, as well as state-level and national-level opinion could be measured, controlled, and manipulated.[42] It required a four-wave panel with three intervening contacts to provide feedback of previous results. It was estimated that 38,400 interviews would be needed among 200 respondents in each of 72 precincts sampled to test for main effects, as well as 28,800 feedback letters. At 1950 prices, conducting this survey would have cost $75,000. Such funding could not be raised then and, allowing for inflation, could not be raised now.

In 1960, researchers investigated how information printed on ballots affected votes cast by a student population.[43] In two of the three treatments the message, "A reliable national poll has recently indicated the following support for the two principal presidential candidates . . .," stated that either John Kennedy or Richard Nixon had a 55 percent to 40 percent lead over the other, with 5 percent undecided. The control group's ballot had no information on it. Although differences appeared among the three groups in the expected directions—those with ballots saying Kennedy was ahead favored Kennedy, for instance—they were not statistically significant. Beyond sample size and the appropriateness of subjects, time may have been a problem: the students had little time to think about the information before making a choice. The electorate, of course, has weeks to evaluate poll results and how they change during the campaign. When there was an active three-way contest in the 1992 campaign, for example, citizens were exposed to frequent readings of how the candidates stood in relation to each other and how their relative standing was changing over time.

A more complex experimental design confronted students with a questionnaire and contrived press releases of results from previous administrations of the same questionnaire.[44] Both their intention to support candidates and issues as well as their images of the candidates and policies changed. However, the result may not have been an illustration of a simple and direct bandwagon effect at work because candidates or issues were reported as having greater than expected shifts in general support, rather than simple majorities. Nevertheless, the approach emphasized the potential significance for some voters of media coverage of polls. Such reporting is especially credible because of the apparent empiricism and objectivity of polls. The analysis usually refers to distinct segments of the population, some of which will inevitably be important for certain audience members. Many voters, especially the uninvolved and those with no strong party affiliation, may be looking to such analyses to help them understand what is going on in a campaign; and these needs would obviously vary by the amount of time left until election day. These same factors suggest limited effects on the politically active, strong partisans, and those with other important groups on which they can rely for information.

In a 1980 experiment, students were divided into groups and told that "a recent public opinion survey of college-educated persons showed Carter [or Reagan] commanding a substantial lead over Reagan [or Carter]."[45] Subsequently, the students were supplied information from a "new Louis Harris poll" and were asked again about their presidential preference using a slightly different form of questioning. In two of three treatments, the information said that either one or the other candidate had a sizable lead; in the third, no statements on candidate dominance were given. Analysis of the results showed that sizable shifts in candidate support and softening of candidate support occurred quickly in the presence of discrepant information, and support declined for the candidate depicted as dominant in the "national poll." Most of the shifting occurred among the undecided and tepid supporters of each candidate. However, the results may have been caused by "oppositional reactivity" rather than an underdog effect because declining support for the dominant candidate was not accompanied by increased support for the opponent.

The most recent study of bandwagon and underdog effects was conducted among registered voters before and after the 1988 presidential election. After manipulating the vote intention question in the preelection survey, the researchers identified apparently simultaneous bandwagon and underdog effects in different subgroups.[46] Employing discriminant analysis, they classified voters in the control group by their candidate preferences and used the resulting function to predict preelection preferences in the treatment group. When the differences between expected and actual preferences were analyzed, one-fifth of the predicted Bush supporters preferred Dukakis, suggesting an underdog effect, while one-tenth of the predicted Dukakis supporters preferred Bush, suggesting a bandwagon effect. The lack of a large net difference in the total sample would have masked these significant countervailing effects. Those who did not make up their minds until late in the campaign were most likely to demonstrate one of these effects.

Another study used contrived news stories to report leads of various sizes for nonpresidential candidates who were otherwise matched in characteristics and were competing in a low-visibility primary election.[47] This "individual effects" study also showed that bandwagon and underdog effects can occur in the same election, affecting different members of the electorate differently. Further research is needed to clarify the conditions under which distinct members of the electorate are affected and in which ways.

There appears, then, to be sufficient theoretical justification for the existence of bandwagon and underdog effects, but that existence is never likely to be demonstrated conclusively because of conceptual difficulties and high costs associated with appropriate research designs. First, the effects are likely to occur simultaneously, so careful designs and analysis would be required to disentangle them. And panel designs would be necessary to measure change whether the work were carried out in the field or in the laboratory.

Exit Polls and Election Night Projections

The potential effects on voters of election day broadcasts of projected outcomes has received considerable research attention since 1964.[48] Before then, there was no coincidence of the use of surveys and unexpected or lopsided outcomes. Network projections, of course, can be made before the polling places are closed on the West Coast because they have increasingly come to be based on exit polls. And the geopolitics of contemporary presidential elections is such that if the Democratic candidate does not accumulate enough electoral votes in states east of the Mississippi, the tabulation of known results will strongly indicate the winner before everyone has had a chance to vote. Many media critics have therefore concentrated on how early predictions of victory in a presidential race might depress turnout in western states and affect the outcome of other races.

A problem with using projections from key precincts arose in the 1964 California Republican primary and a more serious one in the presidential election, when all three networks projected Johnson's victory between 3:48 p.m. and 4:50 p.m. Pacific Standard Time, long before the polls closed on the West Coast.[49] Similarly, in the 1972 election Nixon's widely expected defeat of McGovern was certain shortly after polls closed on the East Coast. The matter became more serious in 1980 when NBC made an early call and President Carter conceded before the polls had closed on the West Coast. The margin of Reagan's victory was somewhat surprising; many pollsters had predicted a relatively close contest.

Since the 1976 presidential election, the networks have used exit polls to make election night projections rather than complicated statistical models using only raw aggregate vote totals from samples of key precincts available when polls have closed. Data collected from voters leaving the polls are available to network analysts throughout the day from both national samples and those in selected states. Because of careful sample designs, the networks now have reliable information about the outcome of the election while voting is still taking place all across the country.

The effects of election night projections have been the object of extensive study since the 1964 election, when the networks appropriated election night as a story uniquely suited to electronic journalism. The tabulation of vote totals became even more rapid when the three networks and the two wire services formed the News Election Service (NES) to collect the raw data on contests for president, senator, representative, and governor.[50] The analysis of the data was, of course, left up to the individual organizations, preserving competition and their editorial independence.

The next step was to collaborate on the conduct of exit polls. Another joint venture, Voter Research & Surveys (VRS), was initiated by ABC, CBS, NBC, and CNN to pool their exit polling operations for the 1990 election. This arrangement was modeled after NES and involved common data collection that saves everyone money. Analyses were again left up to the individual organizations. During the 1990 effort, critics questioned whether the meaning of an election can be interpreted accurately when only one data source is available. For example, the VRS exit poll yielded an estimate that 22 percent of black voters had supported Republican candidates for the House of Representatives. This number was widely publicized by Republican leaders and denigrated by Democrats.[51] The current view is that the estimate was based on a very small sample and was probably not reliable, but the availability of only one estimate may complicate issues of interpreting support for a candidate or party in the future. VRS polls posed another problem of analysis and interpretation in the 1992 Republican primary in New Hampshire. The polling results suggested a very close contest and a major problem for President Bush. The actual vote totals showed a more comfortable Bush margin over Patrick Buchanan. But journalists did not pay as much attention to the vote as they had to the poll in their early coverage of the race.

This is another potential price to pay for the economies of scale created by common data collection. After the 1980 election, observers asked whether the Reagan victory meant the onset of a conservative tide in the electorate that signaled a popular demand for associated policy shifts. Republican pollsters mustered data that suggested the mandate was real, and in its first few months the Reagan administration transformed the mandate into a strong policy initiative. But a more careful reanalysis of multiple data sources has suggested that there was no wholesale shift in the electorate's policy preferences. Support for Reagan reflected dissatisfaction with Carter's performance and the state of the economy rather than the general embrace of a conservative agenda. The exit polls were the basis for the revised interpretation.

The networks argue for their right to collect and disseminate election day information without restraint, while researchers and media critics have cited inadequate aggregate data, relatively weak individual-level data, and faulty logic to demonstrate the harmful effects of the efforts. But the law of minimal consequences says that at best only weak relationships between broadcasts and voters' reactions will be found on election night. Relatively few people are left on the West Coast to be affected by exposure to such information in the last few hours of voting. The effects are more likely to be indirect than direct, and they require a context in which information about the dynamics of the campaign is available right up to election day. For many researchers the central issue has been that "regulating the dissemination of returns on election day should be debated less in terms of the number of votes affected than in terms of the impact on the legitimacy of the electoral process."[52]

Research on the effects of election night projections can initially be divided into studies based on information from aggregate voting returns and those based on information from individual voters. Because of the nature and complexity of possible bandwagon and underdog effects and the likelihood that they offset one another, aggregate voting returns are inherently inadequate for research addressing these issues.[53] But studies analyzing the results of surveys of voters conducted after presidential elections have been unable to present conclusive evidence of substantial effects of projections. Reported relationships have been weak even when they were statistically significant, and the number of voters affected has been very small.

The television coverage of the 1980 presidential campaign has been studied extensively.[54] One study showed that those who were exposed to projections of the presidential election outcome before going to the polls had less propensity to vote. But the conclusions were based on a small number of West Coast voters who met this condition out of 1,814 people from the Center for Political Studies' sample who were reinterviewed between January 8 and 19, 1981. There was considerable difficulty in measuring exposure to media broadcasts so long after the election. The finding that Republicans were less likely than Democrats to turn out after hearing the news suggests an effect detrimental to the leading candidate and his party. But the findings have been sharply criticized by analysts from media organizations.[55]

Public concern about the effects of election night projections has been growing. A 1985 Gallup survey that included an interesting experiment in the phrasing of questions revealed that 72 percent of respondents believed "networks should not report election winners because it discourages voting" (with 18 percent indicating the networks should have the right to report), and 51 percent said the "government should not allow early election projections" (42 percent said the government should not get involved). Thus most people opposed current network practice and would support government efforts to control it.[56]

Controlling election night projections could violate the First Amendment rights of news organizations, however. The networks now operate under a tacit agreement whereby no calls are made of outcomes in a given state until all the polls close there, but the agreement has no legal standing. Some network news people have strongly objected to any compromise with Congress that would apply only to television. Others have felt that an appropriate gesture was necessary to achieve a legislative compromise by which all polls would close at the same time nationally.[57] The House has passed the legislation, but the bill has languished in the Senate since 1988. Passage before the 1992 general election, which seems unlikely, would solve most of the problems associated with election night projections of the outcome of the presidential race, but it would not address similar problems arising in elections for state and other offices.

Polls and the Governing Process

Most evaluations of the impact of polls on contemporary political life focus on their use during campaigns and their effects on voters. But polls also contribute to structuring public opinion on issues and, some argue, guiding the development of policy, especially domestic policy. To some extent the extreme concern that America has a government "of the polls, by the polls, for the polls," can be linked to the increased use of variants on the Gallup question of how well the president is handling his job. Questions now not only focus on the handling of "the economy" or "foreign affairs," but specifically on the handling of the war in the Persian Gulf or relations with Moscow.

Each president since Lyndon Johnson has paid careful attention to public opinion polls, and the White House and the national party committees have devoted increased resources to assembling independent and relatively continuous survey data. Does this increased use of polls portend policy development based on current or expected popular support? No more so than in the past. The increased availability of polling data has not materially affected that process and indeed can often mitigate any such tendencies: "precision journalism is at its best when it is sorting out the conflict among special interest groups, measuring their support, es-timating their potential for having an effect."[58]

For example, people's attitudes on the availability of abortion and support for civil rights generate continual demands for altered policies from organized groups holding very divergent positions. Public debate on these matters has often been illuminated by polling data that suggest the range and intensity of opinions held by the public, political elites, and activists. And survey research has also suggested areas in which particular positions can be staked out, even when one side seems to be nearing a political setback.

Nowhere is this clearer than in the contest over abortion rights and the role of the state in funding abortions under various circumstances. For some time, surveys have shown that a significant majority of men and women supported a woman's right to have an abortion. And pro-choice forces have seized a policy initiative by citing the polls. When the locus of the debate returned to the states after several Supreme Court rulings, an ancillary issue became the conditions under which govern-ment-funded abortion services could be provided to women under age eighteen without parental consent. Here survey data showed the public to be less certain of the appropriate role for government, and opposition to such funding has become the latest rallying point for the pro-life forces.

Thus the reporting of the policy development has been informed by polling, much of it carried out by news organizations. This information has also helped political activists plot strategies and refine them. The public has been provided with relatively continuous feedback on the distribution and stability of views on the issue, at least as it was framed by the wording of questions at the time the surveys were conducted. The use of polls in this instance has provided context and texture to an issue-based debate. There is an analogous role for polls to play in reporting political campaigns: relating the candidates' views on important issues to the distribution of policy preferences in the electorate. But this is a role that the news media seem relatively reluctant to assume.

Conclusion

There is a wide range of documented effects of media polls on the public, some more indirect than others. For those who expected the main effects to be large-scale shifts in voter preference or actual voting behavior based on information about what other citizens are thinking or doing, these effects cannot be demonstrated conclusively. Media polling and reporting of the results of public and private polls can have some salutary effects on public attitudes and behavior. But media critics have been more concerned about possible harmful influences and their consequences for eroding public confidence in the electoral process and the role of news organizations in it.

The impact of public polls varies depending on when in a campaign a poll is taken and the particular part of the electorate under examination. The effects include changing levels of information about who is running for office and their chances of winning, changing levels of interest in the campaign, and changes in willingness to offer money or volunteer time to candidates. Political elites and activists can be affected very differently from the rest of the public. The influences of poll reports on voter preference are likely to be small, although not insignificant in close races, and to offset one another. Demonstrating these influences is difficult for social scientists, however, because designs appropriate to such studies are ill-suited for surveys and best treated in experiments. Such studies must be carefully conducted to ensure controls are properly employed, and they should demonstrate changes in attitudes or behavior that were expected before exposure to poll-based media content.

Sufficient resources will probably never be available to demonstrate conclusively the impact of polls on voter preference and voting behavior, at least not conclusively enough to necessitate changes in public policies controlling media organizations that use polls. And, of course, the First Amendment rights of news organizations cannot be restricted, so the proliferation of media polls is likely to continue as long as these organizations have money to pay for them or to purchase results from syndicated news services.

This limits social and media critics to jawboning to improve the quality of the polls and the reporting of results. The collection and reporting of reliable data in a way that is both scientifically respectable and useful to the public will limit potential harm to voters and to public perceptions of the integrity of the electoral process. In the end, the most critical issue for news organizations may be whether public concern about the media's political coverage, including the use of political polls and election night projections, results in deteriorating support for them as institutions.

Notes

1. Jack W. Germond, "The Impact of Polling on Journalism," in Albert H. Cantril, ed., *Polling on the Issues* (Washington: Seven Locks Press, 1980), pp. 20–27.

2. Floyd Abrams, "Press Practices, Polling Restrictions, Public Opinion and First Amendment Guarantees," *Public Opinion Quarterly*, vol. 49 (Spring 1985), pp. 15-18; and Chanie Kamenetsky, " 'And the Winner Is . . .' Election Day Projections and the First Amendment," *Cardozo Arts and Entertainment Law Journal*, vol. 4 (Spring 1985), pp. 373–400.

3. Kurt Lang and Gladys Engel Lang, *Voting and Nonvoting: Implications of Broadcast Returns before Polls Are Closed* (Waltham, Mass.: Blaisdell Publishing, 1968).

4. Michael W. Traugott, "Public Attitudes about News Organizations, Campaign Coverage, and Polls," in Paul J. Lavrakas and Jack K. Holley, eds., *Polling and Presidential Election Coverage* (Newbury Park, Calif.: Sage Publications, 1990), pp. 134–50.

5. Louis Anthony Dexter, "The Use of Public Opinion Polls by Political Party Organizations," *Public Opinion Quarterly*, vol. 18 (Spring 1954), pp. 53–61.

6. Harrison Hickman, "Public Polls and Election Participants," in Lavrakas and Holley, eds., *Polling and Presidential Election Coverage*, p. 118.

7. See, for example, E. J. Dionne, "Experts Find Polls Influence Activists," *New York Times*, May 4, 1980, p. 26; and Hickman, "Public Polls and Election Participants," pp. 100–33.

8. Larry M. Bartels and C. Anthony Broh, "The Polls—A Review: The 1988 Presidential Primaries," *Public Opinion Quarterly*, vol. 53 (Winter 1989), pp. 563–89.

9. Anthony Downs, *An Economic Theory of Democracy* (Harper, 1957).

10. Jackson Toby, "Are Polls Superior to Primaries for Determining a Party's Best Vote Getter?" *Public Opinion Quarterly*, vol. 20 (Winter 1956), pp. 717–18.

11. Lang and Lang, *Voting and Nonvoting*, p. 90; and Harold deBock, "Influence of In-State Election Poll Reports on Candidate Preference in 1972," *Journalism Quarterly*, vol. 53 (Autumn 1976), pp. 457–62.

12. Irving Roshwalb and Leonard Resnicoff, "The Impact of Endorsements and Published Polls on the 1970 New York Senatorial Election," *Public Opinion Quarterly*, vol. 35 (Fall 1971), pp. 410–14.

13. Thomas R. Marshall, "Evaluating Presidential Nominees: Opinion Polls, Issues, and Personalities," *Western Political Quarterly*, vol. 36 (December 1983), pp. 650–59; Marshall, "The News Verdict and Public Opinion during the Primaries," in William C. Adams, ed., *Television Coverage of the 1980 Presidential Campaign* (Norwood, N.J.: Ablex, 1983), pp. 49–67; and Larry M. Bartels, *Presidential Primaries and the Dynamics of Public Choice* (Princeton University Press, 1988).

14. Henry E. Brady and Richard Johnston, "What's the Primary Message: Horse Race or Issue Journalism?" in Gary R. Orren and Nelson W. Polsby, eds., *Media and Momentum: The New Hampshire Primary and Nomination Politics* (Chatham House, 1987), pp. 127–86.

15. Bartels, *Presidential Primaries*.

16. June O. Yum and Kathleen E. Kendall, "Sources of Political Information in a Presidential Primary Campaign," *Journalism Quarterly*, vol. 65 (Spring 1988), pp. 148–51.

17. Standard sources to consult are Bernard R. Berelson, Paul F. Lazarsfeld, and William N. McPhee, *Voting: A Study of Opinion Formation in a Presidential Campaign* (University of Chicago Press, 1954); and Angus Campbell and others, *The American Voter* (John Wiley, 1960).

18. Steven H. Chaffee and Sun Yuel Choe, "Time of Decision and Media Use during the Ford-Carter Debate" *Public Opinion Quarterly*, vol. 44 (Spring 1980), p. 67.

19. Douglas A. Fuchs and Jules Becker, "A Brief Report on the Time of Day When People Vote," *Public Opinion Quarterly*, vol. 32 (Fall 1968), p. 440.

20. Gladys Engel Lang and Kurt Lang, "The Formation of Public Opinion: Direct and Mediated Effects of the First Debate," in George F. Bishop, Robert G. Meadow, and Marilyn Jackson-Beeck, eds., *The Presidential Debates: Media, Electoral, and Policy Perspectives* (Praeger, 1980), p. 80.

21. David O. Sears and Steven H. Chaffee, "Uses and Effects of the 1976 Debates: An Overview of Empirical Studies," in Sidney Kraus, ed., *The Great Debates: Carter vs. Ford in 1976* (Indiana University Press, 1979), p. 240.

22. See Chaffee and Choe, "Time of Decision and Media Use"; and Margaret K. Latimer, "The Floating Voter and the Media," *Journalism Quarterly*, vol. 64 (Winter 1987), pp. 805–12.

23. Elisabeth Noelle-Neumann, "The Spiral of Silence: A Theory of Public Opinion," *Journal of Communication*, vol. 24 (Spring 1974), pp. 43-51; and Noelle-Neumann, *The Spiral of Silence: Public Opinion—Our Social Skin* (University of Chicago Press, 1984), p. 5.

24. Carroll J. Glynn and Jack M. McLeod, "Public Opinion Communication Processes and Voting Decisions," in Michael Burgoon, ed., *Communication Yearbook*, vol. 6 (Beverly Hills: Sage Publications, 1982), pp. 759–74.

25. Downs, *Economic Theory of Democracy*.

26. Lang and Lang, *Voting and Nonvoting*, pp. 115–20.

27. deBock, "Influence of In-State Election Poll Reports," p. 462.

28. Paul J. Lavrakas, Jack K. Holley, and Peter V. Miller, "Public Reactions to Polling News during the 1988 Presidential Election Campaign," in Lavrakas and Holley, eds., *Polling and Presidential Election Coverage*, pp. 151–83.

29. Richard G. Niemi, Grace Iusi, and William Bianco, "Pre-election Polls and Turnout," *Journalism Quarterly*, vol. 60 (Autumn 1983), pp. 531.

30. See, for example, Herbert Blumer, "Public Opinion and Public Opinion Polling," *American Sociological Review*, vol. 13 (1948), pp. 542–49.

31. Michael Wheeler, *Lies, Damn Lies, and Statistics: The Manipulation of Public Opinion in America* (Liveright, 1976).

32. In addition, the release of the results just before the second presidential debate heavily influenced reporters' expectations of how well Dukakis had to perform to overcome his disadvantage in popular and electoral vote support.

33. Lavrakas, Holley, and Miller, "Public Reactions to Polling News," especially pp. 162–64.

34. Traugott, "Public Attitudes," p. 143.

35. Henry F. Dizney and Ronald W. Roskens, "An Investigation of the Bandwagon Effect in a College Straw Poll Election," *Journal of Educational Sociology*, vol. 35 (1962), p. 109.

36. Eric F. Goldman, "Poll on the Polls," *Public Opinion Quarterly*, vol. 8 (Winter 1944), pp. 461–67.

37. Joseph T. Klapper, "Bandwagon: A Review of the Literature," Office of Social Research, Columbia Broadcasting System (1964), p. 16.

38. David G. Myers, Sandra Brown Wojcicki, and Bobette S. Aardema, "Attitude Comparison: Is There Ever a Bandwagon Effect?" *Journal of Applied Social Psychology*, vol. 7 (October-December 1977), pp. 341–47.

39. Stuart W. Cook and Alfred C. Welch, "Methods of Measuring the Practical Effects of Polls of Public Opinion," *Journal of Applied Psychology*, vol. 24 (August 1940), p. 449.

40. Findings from studies before 1964 have been summarized in Klapper, "Bandwagon," which suggested that this effect may increase as time passes between the election and postelection interviews. Cross-sectional analyses of reported presidential votes in the Center for Political Studies postelection surveys, such as Aage R. Clausen, "Response Validity: Vote Report," *Public Opinion Quarterly*, vol. 32 (Winter 1968), pp. 588–606, and Michael W. Traugott and John P. Katosh, "Response Validity in Surveys of Voting Behavior," *Public Opinion Quarterly*, vol. 43 (Fall 1979), pp. 359–77, demonstrated that the direction of such an effect favored the presidential candidate advantaged by the short-term forces in the campaign. Blair T. Weir, "The Distortion of Voter Recall," *American Journal of Political Science*, vol. 19 (February 1975), pp. 53–62, has also demonstrated the effect. A recent report of a similar finding for "time-based misreporting of the vote for U.S. Senator" that took into account the date of interview in the 1988 CPS Senate Study is Gerald Wright, "Misreports of Vote Choice in the 1988 NES Senate Election Study," paper presented at Electing the Senate Conference, University of Houston and Rice University, 1989.

41. Cook and Welch, "Methods of Measuring the Practical Effects of Polls of Public Opinion," p. 450.

42. Donald T. Campbell, "On the Possibility of Experimenting with the Bandwagon Effect," in Herbert H. Hyman and Eleanor Singer, eds., *Readings in Reference Group Theory and Research* (Free Press, 1968), pp. 452–60.

43. Dizney and Roskens, "Investigation of the Bandwagon Effect."

44. Charles K. Atkin, "The Impact of Political Poll Reports on Candidate and Issue Preferences," *Journalism Quarterly*, vol. 46 (Autumn 1969), pp. 515–21.

45. Stephen H. Ceci and Edward L. Kain, "Jumping on the Bandwagon with the Underdog: The Impact of Attitude Polls on Polling Behavior," *Public Opinion Quarterly*, vol 46 (Summer 1982), pp. 228–42.

46. Lavrakas, Holley, and Miller, "Public Reactions to Polling News," p. 165.

47. Paul J. Lavrakas and Kathy L. Schenck, "Testing of Bandwagon and Underdog Effects Via Fabricated News Stories," paper presented at the 1990 annual conference of the American Association for Public Opinion Research.

48. Warren J. Mitofsky, "A Short History of Exit Polls," in Lavrakas and Holley, eds., *Polling and Presidential Election Coverage*, pp. 83–99.

49. Lang and Lang, *Voting and Nonvoting*.

50. James Brown and Paul L. Hain, "Reporting the Vote on Election Night," *Journal of Communication*, vol. 28 (Autumn 1978), pp. 132–38.

51. E. J. Dionne, Jr., and Richard Morin, "Good News for the GOP—If It's True," *Washington Post National Weekly Edition*, December 17-23, 1990, p. 37.

52. Lang and Lang, *Voting and Nonvoting*, p. xi.

53. For examples of such studies, see Raymond Wolfinger and Peter Linquiti, "Tuning In and Turning Out," *Public Opinion*, vol. 4 (February-March, 1981), pp. 56–60, and Laurily K. Epstein and Gerald Strom, "Election Night Projections and West Coast Turnout," *American Politics Quarterly*, vol. 9 (October 1981), pp. 479–91, which used analysis of aggregate election returns and arrived at different conclusions about West Coast turnout in the 1972 and 1980 elections, respectively.

54. Paul Wilson, "Election Night 1980 and the Controversy over Early Projections," in Adams, ed., *Television Coverage of the 1980 Presidential Campaign*, pp. 141–60.

55. See especially Mitofsky, "Short History of Exit Polls," p. 91.

56. *The People and the Press* (Los Angeles: Times-Mirror, 1986), pp 38–39.

57. Mitofsky, "Short History of Exit Polls," p. 92.

58. Philip Meyer, "Polling as Political Science and Polling as Journalism," *Public Opinion Quarterly*, vol. 54 (Fall 1990), p. 453.

Chapter 7

The Illusion of Technique: The Impact of Polls on Reporters and Democracy

E. J. DIONNE, JR.

THE 1988 and 1992 presidential campaigns produced some of the best arguments ever for the benefits of polling. They were also replete with incidents that led many journalists to conclude that if the press and television really cared about democracy, they would abandon polling altogether.

The strongest argument for polls emerged on the night of March 26, 1988, when Jesse Jackson trounced Michael Dukakis in the Michigan caucuses. Jackson's victory surprised many, but the size of his victory surprised almost everyone. In newsrooms around Michigan, reporters and editors scurried about, asking over and over, what happened? That question will never be answered with certainty because for a variety of reasons—reasons that seemed perfectly valid the day before the caucuses—no major media outlet conducted an exit poll of voters. As a result, questions fundamental to the politics of the 1988 campaign were left unanswered.

Everyone could agree that caucuses were different from primaries and that Jackson, whose supporters were much more fervent than Dukakis's, had benefited from the relatively low turnout. But disagreement about the extent of Jackson's strength could only have been resolved through exit polling. Had Jackson won by drawing an exceptional share of the white vote? Or had black voters all over the state turned out in such large numbers that they dominated the caucuses, voting even in places where whites would normally have been a majority?

In the absence of data, reporters depended on their surmises. They also focused on the Jackson story. So did Democratic party officials, who worried over the prospect of having to deal with a Jesse Jackson far more powerful than they ever imagined. But eleven days later, in the Wisconsin primary, Dukakis trounced Jackson. Jackson drew a respectable share of the white vote but nothing close to the share needed to win.

Jesse Jackson's triumph in Michigan would have been a big story even if exit polls had suggested that there were limits to his appeal to whites. But with exit polls, the story could have been put in some context. At the least, reporters could have answered that question so basic to their craft: What happened?

But if the absence of polls can prove a liability, so can their ubiquitous presence. It is October 1988, after the second presidential debate, and Dukakis trails George Bush in the polls by large margins almost everywhere. Each time the beleaguered Democratic candidate lands in a new city he is surrounded by hordes of local reporters. Their first question is not about war and peace or child care or prosperity. Inevitably it is, "Governor Dukakis, you are running [fill in the number] points behind Vice President Bush in the polls here in [fill in the state]. Is there any way you can catch up?" Dukakis gamely tries to turn the subject to whatever issue he is pushing that day, but the question is repeated in city after city: "Can you win here? Can you catch up? Is the race over?"

In the spring of 1992 President Bush himself, along with Arkansas Governor Bill Clinton, got a taste of the same medicine when Ross Perot emerged at the top of the polls. Why, reporters asked them and their supporters repeatedly, were the two major-party candidates running behind a millionaire who had never held office? What would they do about Perot? (Perot eventually solved their problem by withdrawing from the field in July.)

It is not that the questions posed to Dukakis, Bush, or Clinton were illegitimate. The problem, especially at the end of the 1988 campaign, was that the normal curiosity about who would win an election had become an obsession of such proportions that it threatened to overwhelm any meaningful discussion of the problems that actually engaged voters. Voters were no longer the subjects of politics, democratic citizens deciding the fate of their country. They were objects to be counted, studied, and counted again. The proliferation of polls had allowed almost any newspaper or television station in the nation to measure the feelings of any population. Measurement, not democratic debate, was becoming the stuff of American politics.

"Mind-Forged Manacles"

In the mid-1970s, William Barrett, America's leading interpreter of existentialism, wrote *The Illusion of Technique*, a moving defense of human freedom and an attack on determinism. Barrett opposed what he called a "technology of behavior" and the idea that "the human mind, which creates those techniques of conditioning in the first place, is to be ensnared in the prison of its own devising." He used the evocative phrase of the poet William Blake to refer to the tools through which such conditioning was carried out. He called them "mind-forged manacles."[1]

Have polls become the mind-forged manacles of political reporting in the United States? Much of the reaction against polling stems from the belief that they have. At a most basic and human level, the reaction against polls asserts that human beings are independent, unpredictable, and ultimately immune from the techniques of manipulation. Except perhaps for a few pollsters, almost everyone loves political upsets because they show that human beings refuse to accept the inevitable and loathe the experts who would pretend to know their deepest feelings and inclinations. At some level, then, the war against polls is a war against Barrett's illusion of technique—and that is always to be welcomed.

Related to this critique is another that sees the journalistic obsession with polls and horse race reporting as a flight from substance. This argument, made with particular power by sociologist and social critic Todd Gitlin, contends that reporters are increasingly constrained by the rules of journalistic "objectivity" and by the growing emptiness of American political life. "In the absence of a vital polis, they take polls," Gitlin quipped. He continued,

> In a perverse way, the journalists' fancy for polls is a stratagem toward mastery. Here at least is something they know how to do, something they can be good at without defying their starting premise, which is, after all, deference. Their stance is an insouciant subservience. They have imposed on themselves a code they call objectivity but that is more properly understood as a mixture of obsequiousness and fatalism—it is not "their business" in general to affront the authorities, not "their place" to declare who is lying and who is right. Starting from the premise that they haven't the right to raise issues the candidates don't raise or explore records the candidates don't explore, they can at least ask a question they feel entitled to answer: "Who's ahead?"

"How," he concluded, "can racing addicts be chased away from the track?"[2]

Ted J. Smith III has criticized the media from a very different perspective. He has argued that far from being deferential, journalists have accentuated the negative, not from ideological bias but from their role as "autonomous and neutral critics." The press does not criticize from some particular perspective; it criticizes from everyone's perspective, or perhaps no one's. Journalists can analyze a candidate or a program from the right, the left, or the center without being bound by or accountable to any viewpoint.[3]

Although Smith does not make Gitlin's argument against polls, his analysis fits neatly with Gitlin's critique. If journalists are neutral critics, the path of least resistance in a campaign involves reporting who is up, who is down, and why. They can do this without a hint of ideological bias. They can argue from polls that Dukakis is being hurt by the defense issue or by the liberal label without making a value judgment about his views on defense or about liberalism. Reporters could comment with a basis in statistical knowledge that a campaign commercial in which George Bush appeared with his beautiful blond grandchild was aimed at women and cite as the impetus polls showing that he was being hurt by lack of support from female voters. I should note here that I am not criticizing someone else's work; I made these very points myself during the 1988 campaign and still think they are worth making. But such stories did not promote much discussion about the concerns of women or our society's treatment of children.

Thus a second reason for the attack on polls horse race journalism is apolitical journalism. It highlights technique to the exclusion of substance. It lets reporters off many hooks. Theodore H. White pioneered a form of behind-the-scenes journalism that promoted coverage of the inside story, the moves of the operatives, as well as the outside story, the views and intentions of the candidates. Over time, journalists carried White's lesson much farther than White himself ever did. The inside story overwhelmed the outside story.[4] Polls give a new level of sophistication to inside reporting. Looking at the numbers they generate and the statements and advertisements of the candidates, reporters can know *often even before they talk to the insiders* why a candidate is doing what he is doing and what the insiders themselves are thinking.

The danger, which both Gitlin and Smith point to in different ways, is that journalism gets farther and farther away from what should be its primary purpose: helping democratic citizens make informed decisions and encouraging a wide-ranging democratic debate. Electoral journalism in a democratic society should encourage people to ask, among other things, what do they want the government to do, and who among the candidates is most likely to do it? Instead, as Gitlin has said, journalism focuses increasingly on the surface of things. "Viewers were invited to be cognoscenti of their own bamboozlement." The relevant journalistic question becomes, "How are the candidates trying to do it to us, and how are they doing at it?"[5] The journalism of democracy would promote an active citizenry; the journalism of technique promotes passivity.

A third line of attack on polls accuses them of trying to do with numbers and statistical techniques what reporters ought to do with shoe leather. This turns the traditional argument *for* polls on its head. The news media turned to polls precisely because they realized that there were limits to unscientific door-to-door interviewing. Polls were a check on the tendency of reporters to hear what they wanted to hear and to ignore the rest. Door-to-door interviews could be used not as a source of new information but simply to support the presuppositions of the reporter making the rounds. Many reporters were aware of this danger and avoided it. But even when they were exceptionally scrupulous, they could still never manage to reach 1,500 people around the country. Pollsters could, and their work thus became a useful corrective to the shortcomings of shoe-leather journalism.

But defenders of door-to-door interviewing argue that polls are no substitute for what can be learned through long, unstructured personal conversation. People can be usefully put into the boxes the pollsters create, but they are not limited by those boxes. Only by hearing people out, only by letting voters ask their own questions of themselves, can a reporter truly understand the electorate.

Thus the fundamental lines of criticism on the proliferation of polls. First, polls encourage reporters to endow politics with a scientific quality that it absolutely does not have. Second, polls make it easy for reporters to evade reporting issues and ideas and promote instead a journalism mired in the sophisticated techniques of surveys and advertising. Third, polls take reporters farther and farther away from real people and encourage them to view complex human beings as mere numbers on sheets of computer printout.

There is merit to each of these criticisms. But they need not lead us to abandon polls altogether. The overriding problems that these criticisms point to are the result not of media polls but of long-term changes in the

way our political life is organized and of the misuse of the polls by journalists. The answer to our troubles is not to abandon media polls, but to
put the polls in their place.

Polls as Party Bosses

At the heart of the problems faced by contemporary political journalism
is the decline of political parties. This decline, it should be noted, began
long before media polls were invented. Indeed, the rise of neutral journalism, although a cause of the decline of parties, was also its effect. The
call for the professionalization of reporting was part of the Progressive
Era's general preference for professionalism over politics.[6] As the parties
became weaker after 1900, so did the partisan press. One can welcome
or condemn this development, but it had nothing to do with polling.

One of the paradoxes of American politics is that as the press has
become more professional and less political, its role in electoral politics
has grown. The deterioration in parties and the rise of the direct presidential primary has left to the news media the responsibilities once borne
by party leaders: the media now vet candidates and determine who among
them should be taken seriously. As David Keene, a veteran of Republican
nominating politics, put it, "The people who make the decisions are
different from the ones who made them a few years ago. It used to be
the professional politicians, but today, somebody has to say, 'This fella's
serious and this fella isn't.' A lot of the weight of this decision has fallen
on the press."[7]

This is disturbing to both the politicians and the press because the
question that reporters hate—"Who elected the press?"—becomes increasingly valid if the media begin to shape not only the outcomes of the
electoral process but who gets on the general election ballot. In an effort
to assume this large political role in a professional and apolitical way,
reporters have turned to two seemingly neutral criteria by which to judge
candidates—their character and their standing in the polls. Although the
party leaders also paid attention to character and the polls, they had other
criteria by which to judge their fellow politicians, including ideological
and regional bias and personal friendship. None of these is permitted to
the press.

It is worth noting that ignoring the polls is not necessarily a satisfactory
solution for the press. In 1988 journalists discounted poll findings in
reporting on the candidacies of Bruce Babbitt, Jack Kemp, and Pete du

Pont. All three, especially Babbitt, received far more attention than their poll ratings suggested they deserved because reporters decided that they had interesting things to say. In 1992 many reporters considered Democratic Senator Bob Kerrey a strong candidate even when the polls before the New Hampshire primary told them otherwise. Ignoring the polls is supposed to be a journalistic virtue, but the press came under fire in these instances for making judgments based on subjective criteria. Reporters were accused of bias, especially in their extensive coverage of Babbitt.

The moral is not that we reporters are damned if we do and damned if we don't. Rather, it is that the decline of political parties has thrust reporters into an entirely new role with which we are rarely comfortable. "Objective" criteria, such as the polls, are now being used for purposes for which they were never intended.

The short-term development that so especially affected the 1988 campaign was the lack of any agreement over what the overriding issues facing the country really were. In time of war, economic crisis, or social turmoil, voters have no trouble identifying the key issues and little difficulty in assessing where they, and where the candidates, stand. In 1988, however, the nation's issue agenda, as the pollsters call it, was as diffuse as it has ever been. No one issue—indeed, no group of issues—was paramount. Because there was a vacuum, seemingly minor events and issues—Dukakis's ride in a tank, whether reciting the pledge of allegiance should be required in schools—had much more impact than they would have otherwise.

Although critics of the news media make a fair point when they say that reporters could have done more than they did to fill this vacuum, the vacuum itself was a constraint on journalism. When the country agrees on what the issues are, reporters can comfortably talk and write about them over and over again, knowing there is an audience for what they say. When the issue agenda is so diffuse, so is the audience for stories on issues.

The point is that polling did not create the issue vacuum. Large historical events did. If polls have become more important in political coverage than they were in the recent past, it is for the same reason that Dukakis's ride in the tank was important: it filled part of the vacuum. And if the Dukakis campaign had been more adept at responding to the Bush campaign's charges, its responses would have helped reporters put the polls in their place—and might also have changed what the polls, and the reporters, were reporting.

But reporters, like other human beings, are not the prisoners of broad historical trends like the decline of parties or the lack of a clear issue agenda. They can respond to these developments in a variety of ways. To the extent that journalists use polls to evade reporting on substance, polls are a detriment to journalism. To the extent that polls drive reporters into air-conditioned computer centers and away from the streets, they have led us astray.

By 1992 the issue agenda for the country had become far clearer. The end of the cold war combined with the economic recession to concentrate the country's attention on domestic issues, especially worries about the nation's competitive standing in a new world. The riots in Los Angeles in the spring of 1992 following the verdict finding police officers not guilty of assaulting Rodney King opened a broad debate over how the nation should respond to the continuing degradation of life in its inner cities.

What is striking is that while polls continued to be important in 1992—and not always in productive ways—the relative clarity of the nation's concerns actually did improve the quality of debate, including the quality of journalistic discussion of the issues. Especially during the New Hampshire primary, where voters had access to candidates over a reasonable period of time, the discussion stayed very close to real issues—remarkably so, given the attention in January and early February that focused on Bill Clinton's personal life.

Moreover, after the Los Angeles riots, polls were used to clarify rather than muddle the debate. It mattered, especially to African Americans, that whites polled joined with blacks in rejecting the acquittal of the police officers involved in King's beating. The quality of discussion improved after polls showed that most American rejected a simplistic calculus that either blamed the programs of the 1960s for the riots—a view the Bush White House backed away from almost as soon as it put it forward—or blamed them entirely on the policies of the Reagan and Bush administrations. Polls taken after the riots helped the discussion by showing that Americans were capable of holding a number of ideas at the same time: that the breakdown of families was a problem in the inner city, but so, too, was unemployment; that the welfare system was wasteful, but that the government did have an obligation to help lift up the poor. Most Americans, in short, did not fall into neat boxes labeled liberal and conservative. And what was striking is that on many issues, blacks, whites, and Latinos agreed.

At their best, in other words, polls can explode stereotypes that can be at least as harmful to journalism as the mind-forged manacles of polling itself. The challenge to journalism is to use polls for this purpose and not to substitute poll results for thinking, reporting, and analyzing.

In the end the problem lies less in our polls than in ourselves. The best way to understand the ways the news media misuse polls is to examine why we established polls in the first place.

Answering the Right Questions

The best argument for polls is that they allow journalists to answer questions that we would ask whether the polls existed or not. That may be the single most useful rule in determining whether we are using polls well or badly. Starting with the 1976 election, newspapers and television networks began investing heavily in polls, precisely because they were looking for new ways to answer good questions. While the Gallup and Harris polls usually asked good questions too, they could not possibly ask all our questions, nor did they always ask questions at the moments when we most wanted them answered.

The lack of an exit poll at the Michigan caucuses in 1988 is a good example of how good questions cannot be answered adequately in the absence of the right instruments. We still do not know with the sense of detail we would like how Jesse Jackson pulled off his Michigan victory. And we knew even less on the night of the caucuses, when it really mattered, than we do now, when it matters far less. Those who criticize the news media's fascination with horse race journalism might be moved to ask, so what? Of what importance is it to know how Jackson won in Michigan? Isn't that less important than knowing what Jackson stood for?

The question misses the point. The news media had more or less effectively conveyed what Jackson stood for. What they could not convey in the absence of exit polls was *who* had stood with him in Michigan and *why*. It mattered to the course of the 1988 presidential campaign whether Jesse Jackson and what he stood for were increasingly resonating with white voters. It certainly mattered to Jackson, since he talked repeatedly about how he was creating "common ground" on which blacks and working-class whites could stand together, and referred constantly to his ability to draw both white and black votes. This was not just a personal boast.

The idea that he could create and lead a "rainbow coalition" for social change was the essence of his candidacy. So it really mattered—to *politics*, not just to horse race journalism—what kind of coalition he had assembled in Michigan.

Exit polls, the least controversial of the pollster's instruments, have become indispensable in figuring out the forces that determine the simple clicks in the voting machines. The exit polls did not invent this investigation. Assessing exactly who voted for whom and why is as old as democratic politics itself, because interpreting the meaning of an election can be as important to how the country is governed as the actual vote itself. Exit polls force the interpreters, including reporters, to listen in detail to what the voters are saying. The interpreters cannot simply construe election results any way they choose.

Before the days of reliable exit polls, interpreting the vote was left to Richard Scammon, Samuel Lubell, and other masters of the task of sifting through "key precincts" to understand how Poles or Croatians or blacks had voted. Lubell, one of our nation's most sensitive and hard-working students of voting behavior, would back up his analysis with journeys to neighborhoods across the nation. He would let voters explain for themselves why they were doing what they were doing.

To read Lubell's work is to know that no amount of polling can substitute for real conversations with real voters. But neither can door-to-door interviews over a long period of time substitute for the wealth of illuminating detail that exit polls produce. Indeed, exit polls, interpreted properly, can strengthen the democratic process by allowing reporters to explain what voters are trying to say *at the moment they are saying it*.

Exit polls also allow forms of analysis that were impossible when just key precincts were used. One can roughly know the social characteristics— income and ethnic group, for example—of those who live in a precinct, but one can only guess what the voters who live there think about issues. Exit polls allow analysis not only of which groups voted which way, but also why and what issues influenced them. Moreover, analysis of key precincts allows one to examine the behavior of only the voters who live with other voters like themselves. It misses blacks who live in overwhelmingly white neighborhoods, Jews in gentile neighborhoods, Italians in Irish neighborhoods. Exit polls can measure the views of blacks, Jews, Italians, and others wherever they live.

Here is just a brief list of the things that reporters have been able to conclude through the use of exit polls and why the findings mattered. [8]

—In 1980, John Anderson did well in presidential primaries in Vermont and Massachusetts not because he was popular among Republicans but because he drew strong support from independents who were allowed to vote in those primaries. It was clear that there was an "Anderson phenomenon," but the Anderson phenomenon was not a "Republican phenomenon." Anderson drew the logical conclusion and ran as an independent.

—In 1980, a quarter of the Democrats who said they supported Edward M. Kennedy over Jimmy Carter in the primaries voted for Ronald Reagan in the election. In 1984 a third of Gary Hart's primary supporters backed Reagan instead of Walter Mondale. These results suggested that analyses of voting behavior based on a simple liberal-conservative dichotomy were inadequate. The results also showed the depth of Democrats' disaffection with their party's nominees.

—In 1980, only 11 percent of those who voted for Ronald Reagan said they supported him because he was the "true conservative." This suggested Reagan's ideological mandate was sharply limited.

—Exit polls allow reporters to find out, with some precision, when voters made up their mind to support a candidate. This permits them to know whether seemingly big events actually moved voters. In the Wisconsin Democratic primary in 1980, for example, voters who decided at the last moment strongly supported Carter instead of Kennedy, suggesting that Carter's claim on the morning of the primary that the American hostages in Iran were near release swayed the vote. This was important, since his handling of the hostage issue during the primaries led to considerable resentment on the part of Kennedy's supporters—and came back to haunt Carter on election day when failure to achieve the release probably cost him support.

—In 1980, polls showed that Ronald Reagan's own supporters disagreed with him on his opposition to the Equal Rights Amendment and to abortion. This suggested that Reagan had won *despite* his stand on these issues. But the polls also showed that the minority of voters who said they cast ballots on the basis of the abortion issue voted for Reagan. Thus he probably won in part *because* of the abortion issue. These findings, properly interpreted, provided the basis for a sophisticated view of the influence of the abortion issue in American politics. Pro-life represented the position of a minority, and thus Reagan would have to deal with the issue carefully. But because the pro-life constituency felt more strongly about the issue than the pro-choice constituency did, he would still have political room to speak out against abortion—which he did.

—In 1988, voters who said that maintaining a strong defense was a major issue voted overwhelmingly for George Bush. This not only suggested that the tank ad had worked; it also showed that voter perceptions of Dukakis's weakness on defense issues was more important to his defeat than reporters might have thought if they had not had exit poll data.

—In 1988, if only voters who earned $50,000 a year or less had voted, Bush would still have won the popular vote.[9] This finding emphasized the extent of the Democrats' problems with middle-class voters and set off a lively debate within the party over what it should do to win them back.

—In 1988, Dukakis won two big Southern primaries, Texas and Florida, largely because of his strength among voters who were not stereotypically Southern—notably northern transplants in Florida and Hispanics in Texas. His potential strength among Hispanics was largely realized in November; but polls also pointed to his weaknesses among the kind of white Southern Democrats who had defeated northern liberal nominees in the past. They would beat Dukakis, too. Thus his potential weaknesses were revealed early, even when he was doing well, and they could have tipped reporters to his weaknesses in November.

—Patrick J. Buchanan ran a fervently conservative ideological campaign against President Bush in 1992 and won a third of the vote or more in the early primaries. But was support for Buchanan mostly a protest against Bush's policies by the Republican right wing? The exit polls made clear that it was not. Buchanan did about as well among liberal and moderate Republicans as among conservatives. Exit polls showed that voters' concern for a weak economy and their own shaky economic circumstances had more to do with their support for Buchanan than how they labeled themselves ideologically.

—In 1992, Paul Tsongas received strong support, especially in the Connecticut and New York primaries, even after he had dropped out of the race. Did this mean voters were embracing his message on the economy? Only to a limited degree, the polls suggested. In fact, many of the votes for Tsongas were cast in protest against the other two candidates left in the field, Clinton and former California Governor Jerry Brown.

—In 1992, exit polls in state after state implied that the old liberal, moderate, and conservative labels had little to do with how Democratic primary voters cast their ballots, suggesting that political reporters (and academic analysts) needed to come up with new frameworks to understand divisions within the Democratic party.

—In 1992, in almost all states women cast a substantial majority of the votes in Democratic primaries, while men made up a majority in most of the Republican primaries. This fact would be impossible to know without exit polls, and it shed useful light on some of the important developments of 1992, notably the victories of Lynn Yeakle of Pennsylvania, Carol Moseley Braun of Illinois, and Barbara Boxer and Dianne Feinstein of California in U.S. Senate primaries. (The polls also showed women candidates winning strong support among men, suggesting that women candidates were profiting from more than gender solidarity.)

No doubt a critic of polls could list cases in which reporters interpreted exit polls misleadingly. But because poll results are now widely available, and because many news organizations now use the same polls, provided by the Voter Research and Surveys consortium, there is a check on distortion.

What emerges from this list may be two other rules that ought to apply to journalistic polling analysis: first, polls are most valuable in challenging and overturning preconceptions; second, polls should be used to describe the complexity of public opinion, not to oversimplify what citizens think.

Detailed analysis of polls has been especially valuable in clarifying exactly where the public stands on abortion. When people are asked questions about abortion, they are often ambivalent. There is no single majority on abortion; there are, at minimum, two overlapping majorities. When pollsters ask whether choices of individual women or government policy should be binding, the response is overwhelmingly pro-choice. Citizens are uneasy about government interference with intimate decisions. Yet when the question is posed differently, pollsters get a different result: most of the country thinks too many abortions are performed, rejects many of the reasons women give for having abortions, and favors certain restrictions such as requiring teenagers to get parental permission.[10]

Such poll findings have greatly influenced strategists in both the pro-choice and pro-life movements and may actually have improved public discussion on the matter. The pro-choice movement has taken to emphasizing that it wants fewer abortions. A popular pro-choice slogan now is that abortion should be "safe, legal, and *rare*." Many pro-choice advocates also emphasize their support for better access to birth control and for prenatal and postnatal care as a way of making it easier for women to choose to give birth, if that is what they really wish. Some elements of the pro-life movement have begun to favor less than an all-encompassing ban on abortion and have emphasized the personal, moral character of the abortion decision, instead of the political battle for and against restrictions.

There are many other issues on which the public resists being pigeonholed, but it is only possible to know this if those taking polls are concerned with understanding the complexity of public opinion. A series of surveys commissioned by the Times-Mirror Company has admirably attempted to gauge public opinion properly by posing different questions exploring related issues. Thus, a 1987 Times-Mirror survey found that 66 percent of Americans rejected the idea that "women should return to their traditional role in society." Yet 68 percent also said that "too many children are being raised in day-care centers" and 87 percent said they had "old-fashioned values about family and marriage."[11] What one can learn here is that Americans are, in a sense, both feminist and traditionalist. They welcome improved opportunities for women yet worry about what is happening to the family and to public morality. Americans are not sexist or blue-nosed, but neither are they permissive.

The same survey found that 71 percent of Americans said "government should take care of people who can't take care of themselves" and 62 percent said "government should guarantee every citizen enough to eat and a place to sleep." Yet only 29 percent agreed with the statement that "hard work offers little chance of success" and only 38 percent agreed that "success in life is pretty much determined by forces outside our control." Americans, in other words, believe simultaneously in compassion and self-reliance. Similarly, a 1977 *New York Times*/CBS News poll found that even among Americans who favored a guaranteed annual income for the needy, a majority expressed disapproval for welfare programs.[12] Such polls can be interpreted in many ways: they suggest most notably the stigma that attaches to the word "welfare." But what they show above all is that we should be wary of parodying public opinion. Polls, properly used, can help fight the tendency to oversimplify the public's attempt to reach judgments on public issues.

Polls and Democracy

Two other criticisms of polling's impact on journalism deserve special attention.

The first is the charge that polls create opinion out of whole cloth. On many issues people have not fully thought through exactly what they think, do not have enough information, or feel ambivalent. The danger is that pollsters may ask a question that the respondent has never thought much about. Most of the time, respondents, being polite, will offer one answer or another, but as often as not, the opinion being expressed is held only for the moment of the interview. There are many ways around this problem, notably by trying to determine how much a respondent knows or cares about a particular issue and by asking multiple questions in search of consistencies and inconsistencies. But too often that is not done. Journalistic pollsters need to avoid forcing respondents to take sides before they are ready. In the normal course of events (not just in polling), journalists should make respondents comfortable in saying "I don't know" when that is what they really want to say. (The practice of admitting a lack of knowledge or the absence of a fully thought-out opinion might also be usefully encouraged among journalists themselves, as well as among academic commentators.)

The second criticism, made by political theorist Benjamin R. Barber, is that at times polls simply invite respondents to express private prejudices and thus "give prejudice public standing and reinforce its legitimacy."[13] Although measuring prejudice can be a useful exercise, Barber suggests that if the goal is to assess what public judgments citizens are reaching, polls can take respondents through the various arguments on a particular issue. His goal is to encourage attention to how people's opinions change as they are given more information or asked to examine an issue from its various sides.

The most difficult problem for journalistic polling, raised notably by the political commentator Christopher Hitchens, involves the ways in which polls themselves affect not only journalism but the entire democratic process.[14] Among the most recent innovations is the use of the tracking poll, which measures day-to-day changes in public opinion. Tracking polls can be exceptionally useful, which is why political campaigns that can afford them use them as much as possible. They can also help journalists avoid serious errors. Gary Hart won the 1984 Democratic primary in New Hampshire after coming in second in the Iowa caucuses. Iowa had drawn public attention to him and helped identify him as the candidate with the best chance of defeating Walter Mondale. As a result, many anti-Mondale voters shifted from other candidates (notably Senator John Glenn of Ohio) to Hart. Journalists with access to tracking polls understood what was going on, but some who did not have access to these polls failed to catch the trend.

One result of the 1984 experience is a near obsession with tracking polls, a result especially visible during the 1992 New Hampshire primary. The *Boston Globe*, in cooperation with WBZ-TV in Boston, conducted extensive and admirably accurate tracking polls that proved very useful in tracing the rise of Paul Tsongas and in detailing the impact of reports about Bill Clinton's personal life and draft record on his standing. To their credit, these news organizations permitted wide access to their data. Still, it is legitimate to ask if reporters' interest in the tracking polls may have pushed coverage toward the Tsongas-Clinton dynamic and away from covering their differences on issues—and also from differences among Clinton, Tsongas, and the other contenders. In the end, the use of tracking polls may have helped make New Hampshire into a two-person race. They may also have increased the coverage of the personal issues that swirled around Clinton by making it easy for journalists to gauge his rise, fall, and partial resurrection.[15]

The Clinton forces themselves made brilliant use of what might be called the "tracking poll effect." In the end Clinton won 26 percent of the vote in the primary, losing to Tsongas by 9 percentage points. Yet he beat Tsongas to the television cameras and proclaimed himself "the comeback kid"—a phrase that stuck—because his 26 percent was higher than his low point in the tracking polls of 19 or 20 percent. (Conservative commentator Pat Buchanan also enjoyed a good election night because early exit polls showed him getting more than 40 percent of the vote in his race against President Bush, even though, when the write-in votes were counted, he had won only 37 percent.)

Should news media tracking polls be abandoned? No, especially because campaigns conduct such polls themselves and leak the results and because having public benchmarks can be useful for journalist and citizen alike. But there is certainly good reason to examine how tracking polls can distort coverage and encourage horse race reporting even more. Tracking polls are best used as a check on other sources, and on journalist's fallible instincts.

The rise of Ross Perot's independent candidacy in the spring of 1992 raised an even larger question for journalistic polling. The interest Perot generated through his early television appearances was clear enough, given the apparent outpouring of volunteers ready to put his name on the ballot. He instantly tapped a deep unease with the status quo. Yet his rise—and his subsequent fall—was also facilitated by national polls. Once a public poll appeared showing Perot leading both President Bush and Bill Clinton, he became a contender on a par with the candidates who had struggled through a series of primaries to win their party nominations. In effect, national polls became a substitute for the entire party apparatus.

Perot himself, with his talk of "electronic town halls," seemed to have more faith in the possibilities of polling than many pollsters themselves. (Ironically he pulled out of the race after polls began to measure the second thoughts voters had about him.) His experience dramatizes the extent to which polls must be seen not as mere instruments, but as institutions that can powerfully affect the entire democratic system.

Rethinking the ways journalists use polls is especially important at a moment when Americans have doubts about the efficacy of democracy and wonder whether journalists are more part of the problem than of the solution. A fundamental flaw in American democracy as now practiced is the tendency of political campaigns to view voters as mere collections of impulses to be stroked and soothed. Many of the institutions that used to give voters a sense of connection to the political process—party organizations, trade unions, neighborhood groups—face severe challenges.

Reporters' use of polling fails them if it encourages a static view of politics that leaves out public deliberation and thoughtful persuasion. To the extent that polling makes citizens experience politics as a manipulative game in which their only role is be studied and counted, it is not doing democracy any favors.

But this is not the only use of polls. Polls can explode journalistic prejudices and preconceptions. They can answer legitimate questions that could not otherwise be answered. Done well they can provide a complex view of how citizens reason, separately and together, about public problems. Polls can be the servants of journalism and democracy. But only if they are viewed that way.

Notes

1. William Barrett, *The Illusion of Technique* (Anchor Books, 1979), especially pp. xi–xiiv.

2. Todd Gitlin, "Blips, Bites, and Savvy Talk: Television's Impact on American Politics," *Dissent*, vol. 37 (Winter 1990), pp. 18–19.

3. Ted J. Smith III, "The Watchdog's Bite," *American Enterprise*, vol. 1 (January–February 1990), pp. 62–70.

4. This point is made notably by Richard Brookhiser, *The Outside Story: How Democrats and Republicans Re-elected Reagan* (Doubleday, 1986).

5. Gitlin, "Blips, Bites, and Savvy Talk."

6. A useful look at the development of the nonpartisan press is Michael Schudson, *Discovering the News: A Social History of American Newspapers* (Basic Books, 1978).

7. David Keene, interview with author.

8. The poll results cited here for 1980, 1984, and 1988 are largely from *New York Times/CBS News* polls. The 1992 results are from polls conducted for a consortium of networks and news organizations by Voter Research and Surveys.

9. The datum on Bush winning among voters who earned less than $50,000 a year became central to postelection debates among Democrats about the future of their party. It was deployed most notably by William Galston and Elaine Ciulla Kamarck, *The Politics of Evasion: Democrats and the Presidency* (Washington: Progressive Policy Institute, 1989).

10. On abortion polls, see E. J. Dionne, Jr., *Why Americans Hate Politics* (Simon and Schuster, 1992), pp. 341–42.

11. Dionne, *Why Americans Hate Politics*, pp. 325–26.

12. E. J. Dionne Jr., "The New Politics of Jobs," *Public Opinion*, vol. 1 (March–April 1978), pp. 50–55.

13. Benjamin R. Barber, "Opinion Polls: Public Judgment or Private Prejudice," *Responsive Community*, vol. 2 (Spring 1992), pp. 4–6.

14. Christopher Hitchens, "Voting in the Passive Voice: What Polling Has Done to American Democracy," *Harper's*, April 1992, pp. 45–52.

15. I speak here not in criticism of others but of my own second thoughts, since I was among the most eager journalistic consumers of the *Globe*/WBZ-TV polls.

Index